Cambridge Elements

Elements in Histories of Emotions and the Senses
edited by
Rob Boddice
Tampere University
Piroska Nagy
Université du Québec à Montréal (UQAM)
Mark Smith
University of South Carolina

MEDIEVAL AVATARS

Projecting Presence, Performing Emotions

Carla Maria Bino
Catholic University of the Sacred Heart

Shaftesbury Road, Cambridge CB2 8EA, United Kingdom

One Liberty Plaza, 20th Floor, New York, NY 10006, USA

477 Williamstown Road, Port Melbourne, VIC 3207, Australia

314–321, 3rd Floor, Plot 3, Splendor Forum, Jasola District Centre,
New Delhi – 110025, India

Cambridge University Press is part of Cambridge University Press & Assessment,
a department of the University of Cambridge.

We share the University's mission to contribute to society through the pursuit of
education, learning and research at the highest international levels of excellence.

www.cambridge.org
Information on this title: www.cambridge.org/9781009610742

DOI: 10.1017/9781009610759

© Carla Maria Bino 2026

This publication is in copyright. Subject to statutory exception and to the provisions
of relevant collective licensing agreements, no reproduction of any part may take
place without the written permission of Cambridge University Press & Assessment.

When citing this work, please include a reference to the DOI 10.1017/9781009610759

First published 2026

A catalogue record for this publication is available from the British Library

ISBN 978-1-009-61074-2 Hardback
ISBN 978-1-009-61073-5 Paperback
ISSN 2632-1068 (online)
ISSN 2632-105X (print)

Cambridge University Press & Assessment has no responsibility for the persistence
or accuracy of URLs for external or third-party internet websites referred to in this
publication and does not guarantee that any content on such websites is, or will remain,
accurate or appropriate.

For EU product safety concerns, contact us at Calle de José Abascal, 56, 1°, 28003
Madrid, Spain, or email eugpsr@cambridge.org

Medieval Avatars

Projecting Presence, Performing Emotions

Elements in Histories of Emotions and the Senses

DOI: 10.1017/9781009610759
First published online: February 2026

Carla Maria Bino
Catholic University of the Sacred Heart

Author for correspondence: Carla Maria Bino, carla.bino@unicatt.it

Abstract: This Element explores how medieval devotional and disciplinary practices acted as 'immersive technologies' for producing presence and configuring emotions. Through the comparative analysis of Aelred of Rievaulx's *De Institutione Inclusarum* and the *Ordo ad Faciendum Disciplinam* of the lay confraternity of Santo Stefano in Assisi, it investigates how the devout subject projected themselves into an imaginal, affective space, where memory, posture, and sensory experience converged to enable a participatory encounter with the divine. Drawing on the concept of the 'avatar' as a psychosomatic projection of the self within visionary and ritual practices, the Element traces how the 'theatre of the mind' redefined the relationship between interior vision, exterior action, and affective identity. By examining the dramaturgies of presence articulated within these memorial plays, this Element sheds light on the role of sensory discipline and emotional posture in shaping embodied devotional experience in the Latin Middle Ages.

Keywords: avatar, presence studies, medieval drama, performance studies, theory of representation

© Carla Maria Bino 2026

ISBNs: 9781009610742 (HB), 9781009610735 (PB), 9781009610759 (OC)
ISSNs: 2632-1068 (online), 2632-105X (print)

Contents

1 Avatars within the Theatre of the Mind — 1

2 Projecting Presence: 'Becoming' Magdalene — 20

3 Performing Emotions: Feeling Like the Mother — 34

4 Epilogue — 53

References — 58

1 Avatars within the Theatre of the Mind

1.1 Prologue

This Element reflects on two texts that are markedly different in historical context, form, and function: the *De institutione inclusarum*, written by the monk Aelred of Rievaulx for his sister, an anchoress (1160–1162), and the *Ordo ad faciendum disciplinam* (sic) of the Confraternity of the Flagellants of Santo Stefano in Assisi, affiliated with the city's Franciscan convent (1327–1329). The former is a rule composed by a Cistercian monk for a woman who had entirely withdrawn from the world and dedicated her life to the love of Christ; the latter is a ritual likely authored by a Franciscan friar for a lay male association embedded in the civic sphere, whose aim was the practice of charitable works.

What links these two texts, and why do they matter?

Both shed light on the dynamics through which the devout accessed an imaginative experience, enabling a tangible and participatory encounter with the divine. Although the dynamics differ radically (indeed, they are almost inverse), both foreground a close interplay between the sensory and emotional experience directed outward to the material texture of daily life, and that which turns inward towards the spiritual domain of imaginative devotion, whether meditative or ritual in form.

In the first case, the rule Aelred offers his sister seeks to direct her vocation of enclosure by harmonising the 'outward' customs of the body, lived out in the daily solitude of the cell, with the 'inward' posture of the soul, oriented solely towards the love of God. This harmony is continuously shaped through a meditative exercise that begins from the memory of Christ's life, vividly re-enacted and relived by the woman within her mind.

In the second case, the devotion of the Assisi brethren is an 'esoteric' lay liturgy (private, exclusive, and immersive) which the group celebrates at Vespers on Good Friday. On this occasion, they gather within the enclosed space of their oratory, don the confraternal habit, and 'enter' into a ritual through which they memorialise Christ's Passion: first mentally re-enacting it, then reliving it bodily through acts of self-flagellation and weeping. This ritual exercise – statutorily prescribed and mandatory – constitutes the very foundation of the sodality and serves as the generative core of their exoteric practices (public, social, and communal acts) that stem from the brethren's obligations. In both cases, the processes of sensory and emotional perception unfold through a dynamic of exterior-interior, of closure-openness – one that involves not only the physical dimensions of space and time, but also the individual itself, articulated according to the dual logic of *homo exterior* (body) and *homo interior* (soul).

Much has been written on the relationship between the senses of the mind and those of the body in the medieval experience of vision – both of immaterial and of material images. I am thinking, for instance, of the work of Hamburger (1998, Hamburger and Bouché 2006), Newman (2005), and Karnes (2011), and more recently of that of Largier (2022) and Van't Spijker (2004, 2022), to mention those whose contributions have most influenced my own thinking.

My perspective, however, is dramaturgical – one might even say processual and functional. I am interested in examining how the exterior-interior and closure-openness dynamic influences the construction of imaginative experience; how, the latter, in turn, reshapes the subject's sensory and emotional perception. This reciprocal movement re-forms a new psychosomatic identity (*how* the subject redefines their relationship to the divine and to other human beings). In the examples I consider, this dynamic appears to be at once oppositional and complementary.

It is oppositional insofar as imaginative experience requires two necessary conditions. First, the devotee must withdraw from the external world and enter an enclosed space (the cell, the oratory). Second, by isolating itself from its surroundings, the body itself becomes an 'experiential site': it opens an inner space of vision and becomes the medium for an alternative form of perception. In other words, imaginative vision requires two closures: enter an enclosed space to shut the world *out*, then close the senses to that world, turning wholly to the immaterial *within*. Then, the eyes and senses of the body must *close* themselves *off* from material reality and reorient entirely towards an immaterial, 'other' reality that unfolds within the interior domain. Thus, imaginative experience rests on a twofold physio-sensory movement: a withdrawal and closing off from the outside, and a simultaneous opening and entry into the inside.

The exterior-interior dynamic is also complementary, in that external conditions help shape the imaginative experience itself. Both the configuration of the visionary space and the structure of the vision are influenced by several factors: the physical environment in which the devotee's body is situated (filled with objects, sounds, and images); the texts used in prayer or meditation; the gestures and actions of the ritual; and the specific time or circumstance in which the inner space is opened. Environmental contingencies and temporal circumstances each help shape imaginative experience. They also influence how the devotee projects themself into the inner space and – through a process of sensory introflexion, which turns perceptual and emotional faculties back upon themselves – generate an 'imaginal' presence of their own real, physical body.

Conversely, the way the imaginal body inhabits the imaginative space – how it perceives, acts, and is acted upon – has effects on the real body, influencing outward attitudes, behaviours, and relationships. Imaginative experience thus functions as a training ground for the senses and emotions: a perceptual exercise that disciplines the subject and gradually forms a consonant unity between *intus* and *foris* – an inner-outer coherence that becomes a way of living.

This Element investigates what remains constant – and what shifts – in the process by which imaginative experience is formed across its two case studies. It does so by examining the formative process itself: the physical-sensory closure to the external world, the sensory-emotional opening of an inner space, and the production of an imaginal body through which the devotee projects presence into the vision. I show how shifts in the conditions and circumstances of imaginative experience generate distinct dramaturgies of inner representation. These shifts also reshape the sensual and emotional relations between the devotee's real body and their imaginal one.

I call the devotee's imaginal body an *avatar* – that is, a production of the subject's own presence and a projective relocation of their sensory and emotional faculties. The avatar is experienced by the devotee as their own 'personal body', a fully sensitive corporeal form. Through this body they inhabit the imaginative experience, seeing, acting, speaking, relating, and therefore feeling and being affected emotionally in the first person.

I use the term *memorial play* for imaginative experience because it is an active act of image-making, one that takes memory as its instrument and mnemotechnics as its craft. As Carruthers (1990, 1998) has shown, this process is fundamentally participatory. The images composed by the devotee in their mind are not static tableaux to be viewed frontally; rather, they are three-dimensional, living scenes in which the devotee takes part. Within them, the subject engages directly with the surrounding environment and with the objects encountered, as well as with other figures, experiencing concrete physical sensations and distinct emotional responses. The ordered sequence of these scenes forms a performance played by the devotee as a real, sensual experience.

Finally, I call *theatre of the mind* the inner space in which imaginative experience takes shape. This is not a metaphor of my own invention, nor do I employ the term 'theatre' in either its classical sense or its later, post-Renaissance – and fully modern – sense.

The *theatre of the mind* has theoretical foundations that can be traced back to Tertullian and was more fully systematised by Augustine. It is understood metonymically as the foremost of the *spectacula christianorum* – those spectacles offered by Christian apologists and Church Fathers in opposition to the *ludi* of the Roman Empire, which they categorically rejected. Yet this was not a new form of material spectacle. Rather, it constituted a radically different *way of seeing*, one fundamentally opposed to the pagan model. It corresponded to a dispositive of dramatic, first-person knowledge that the Fathers anchored in the epistemological principles of Christian thought.

I use the term *dispositive* – in the Foucauldian sense of the *dispositif* (Foucault 1994: 299–300) – to denote a strategy of vision that shifts the spectator's viewpoint from outside the scene to within it, disciplining the gaze according to a logic of action that reverses the logic of passive consumption. The shift from a 'spectatorial' and bystanding 'seeing' to a 'dramatic' and actant 'seeing' entails a redefinition of both representational processes and perceptual dynamics. On the representational front, vision is no longer conceived as analogical or fictional, but as re-actualising – an iteration or intensification of presence. On the perceptual front, dramatic vision entailed a psychosomatic engagement that went far beyond synaesthesia: it involved the individual as a whole, with no separation between *intus* and *foris*, soul and body, emotions, senses, and behaviours.

From the anti-spectacular revolution theorised by the Church Fathers – which I have described as a "dramatic turn" (Bino 2023) – and from the elaboration of the dramatic dispositive, there emerged a new conception of theatre shifted entirely onto participation and immersion. This shift brought with it a resemanticisation of key terms such as *repraesentare, agere, fingere, simulare*, and *imitare*.

This idea constitutes a structural and inescapable cornerstone of Christian thought. It contributes to the historical and epistemological grounding of the contemporary category of performance, a concept widely (and often over-) used in medieval studies. Today, performance functions as a methodological principle not only in research on the visual culture of the Christian West (Starkey and Wenzel 2005), but also in major contributions to the cultural history of the senses (Newhauser 2014), the historical anthropology of emotions (Morrison and Bell 2013, Rosenwein 2015, Boquet and Nagy 2018), devotional, meditative, and homiletic literature (Muessig 2002, Steenbrugge 2017, Dutton and Kirakosian 2023), and public and private practices of reading and prayer (Starkey 2004, Brantley 2007, Gertsman 2008). In particular, the notion of performance has become a key interpretive paradigm in image theory and art history. These fields have drawn attention to the agentive potential of images. Scholars have emphasised how perception was shaped by the physical and material properties of images – understood both as sensory, tactile qualities and as tangible manifestations of abstract concepts (Nelson 2007, Pentcheva 2010, Flora 2010, Bynum 2011, 2020, Kessler 2019, Jørgensen *et al.* 2023). Although grounded in different historical-critical premises, these lines of research all point to the persistence of a performative model of representation – often encapsulated in the notion of 'experience'. This applies both to studies on the meaning of embodied gestures and to actions within ritual and liturgy (Palazzo 2014), and to more recent work on the role of emotion in devotional practice (Stevenson 2010, Gertsman 2015), or on the affective dimension of meditative, contemplative, and mystical vision (McNamer 2010, Johnson 2019, Mancia 2019, Sanmartín Bastida 2023). In these approaches, scholars consistently highlight the agency of an embodied gaze. This gaze is not abstract, but spatially and temporally situated. It possesses a tangible, almost personal presence, capable of interacting with the elements of a scene that is sensory, dynamic, and operative.

I will begin by outlining the key moments in the patristic development of the dramatic dispositive, highlighting its consequences for the sensory and emotional perception of divine and worldly experience.

It is on this theoretical ground that I will base my reading of the two examples under consideration.

1.2 The Dramatic Turn: Seeing from Within

The first formulation of the dramatic dispositive of vision emerged between the second and fifth centuries, within what Lugaresi (2008) has termed "the Christian discourse on spectacles". This was not a moral condemnation of the pagan *ludi*, nor a polemic against their content. Rather, it was an epistemological and gnoseological reflection on the relationship between being and appearance, truth and falsehood, likeness and simulation – issues that had been reconfigured by the personal nature of the God-Truth and by the Incarnation, a paradoxical unity of the invisible and the visible.[1] That discourse, though rooted in Late Antiquity, developed into a powerful ideological framework that opposed *spectacularity* and continued to influence Christian thought well into the early modern era. The Church Fathers – especially Tertullian, Origen, Lactantius, and Augustine – explored *how*, and *through what means* human beings could come to see and know the truth of God, made accessible through the incarnate Logos. This divine Word entered the world, acted in history, and revealed the unity of the divine economy of creation.

---

[1] The personal nature of truth in Christianity has no precedent in any other philosophical, religious, or mythological system (Ferri 2007: 17–18). The Incarnation compels a shift from asking "what is truth?" (*quid est veritas?*) – a question that seeks objective, ontological knowledge (the *quid*) – to asking "who is truth?" (*quis est veritas?*). In the New Testament, truth is conceived as a dynamic and operative concept, constituted by actions and relationships: it is only by 'doing the truth' (that is, practicing it) that one comes to know it – just as a *quis*, a personal subject, is known only through encounter (Penna 2002: 219).

The core premise is this: because revealed truth is indivisible, spectacle proves inadequate as a dispositive for knowledge. By its very nature, it is double: it entails both a separation between *what is* and *what appears* produced by fictional mimesis, and a distancing of the spectator, who remains removed from what is seen and alienated from it.

The *duplicitas* of the spectacular dispositive unfolds across three distinct visual processes, each producing sensory, emotional, and behavioural effects on the viewer. These are explained through analogies with the imperial *ludi* (*circenses, scaenici,* and *munera*), whose impact on the audience is encapsulated in the well-known Christian formula "*spectacula furiosa, vel cruenta vel turpia*", widely echoed throughout the later tradition. The circus spectacle is a visual process grounded in illusion: it releases uncontrollable impulses (*furor*) that overwhelm perception and stir irrational desire for what is *vanitas* – a deceptive stand-in for the desire for *veritas*. The theatre spectacle is a visual process that functions through simulation and generates 'deformity' (*turpitudo*): it alters reality so powerfully that it severs *being* from *appearance*, dulls sensory responsiveness, and deforms perception and conduct. Lastly, the amphitheatre spectacle is a visual process driven by distance and results in inhumanity (*crudelitas*): the physical, legal, and social separation between those in the arena and those watching from the stands becomes almost ontological, enabling the spectator to derive pleasure from the suffering and death of someone perceived as radically other.

These three visual processes demonstrate that the spectacular dispositive is not only an inadequate gnoseological device, but also a dangerous one. Rooted in illusion, simulation, and distance, it produces a gaze that is blind, distorted, and remote, incapable of distinguishing *what is* from *what merely appears*. The result is a collapse of discernment that appearance comes to replace truth, with the illusory displacing the real.

From a perspectival error, spectacle becomes a *cognitive tension* fundamentally opposed to revealed truth and intimately bound up with desire and emotion. Tertullian (*De Spectaculis* 14–15) counts spectacle among the pleasures of the flesh (*voluptas concupiscentiae*), which shatter the integrity of the soul (*concussio spiritui*). By contrast, Lactantius (*Divinae Institutiones* 6:20) sees it as an endless visual pleasure (*voluptas*), one that binds the senses to their object. Augustine makes a decisive contribution to the nexus of spectacle, knowledge, and desire – one that will prove foundational for the anthropology of Western Christianity. Spectacle, he argues, satisfies a specific form of desire, which he defines as the lust for spectacle (*cupiditas spectaculi*) or the greed of the eyes (*concupiscentia oculorum*). Both definitions are brought together in the term *curiositas*, which designates a desire to know and to understand that remains confined to what is visible and perceptible – that is, to mere appearances. Alongside sensual pleasure (*desiderium voluptatis*) and the ambition to excel (*ambitio excellentiae*), *curiositas* is one of the three desires that constitute the love of the world (*dilectio mundi*): a love defined as *diligere ad beatitudinem* – a self-enclosed enjoyment that seeks fulfilment in its own gratification. According to Augustine, this is the only form of love available to human beings after their fall, when they chose to rebel against God and were cast far from him. Since then, as Augustine explains, the human being has desired and loved the world independently of God, because from a distance he can no longer see that the world is created, nor recognise that he himself is made in the likeness of the divine image. Christian revelation identifies this kind of love for the world as *adulterinus* – at once a betrayal of God, in which the human being replaces the Creator with his creatures, and a corruption of the divine image in which humanity was made (*In Epistolam Ioannis ad Parthos* 2:11–13). The three desires of the world have sight in common – metonymically, Augustine takes sight to stand for the whole of human perceptual capacity (*Confessiones* 10:35:54; *Sermo 112*, 7). What drives this capacity towards earthly things and holds it fast to them is an *affectus* misdirected by the *voluntas*; it turns the human tension for knowledge into 'scopophilia', or 'spectacularity' – a love of visibilities (Bino 2015: 56–59). When a perverse *voluntas* generates inverted *affectus* (Boquet 2005: 86), these in turn produce 'perverse imitations' of the love of God, which the human subject keeps at a distance:

> Pride apes what is sublime; ... Tender blandishments are meant to stir up love. ... Curiosity passes itself off as zeal for knowledge; ... Thus, the soul fornicates when it turns from you and looks beyond you for pure and lucid intentions, which are found only by turning back to you. In a distorted way all humankind imitates you, yet they set themselves far from you and raise themselves against you (*Perverse te imitantur omnes, qui longe se a te faciunt et extollunt se adversum te*). (*Confessiones* 2:6:13)

For Augustine, perverse imitation is simulation: it is hypocrisy – the deliberate split between being and seeming, *intus* e *foris*. In sum, the spectacular dispositive concerns perception, desire, and action. It is a remote, outward mode of seeing that sets a misdirected affective process in motion and culminates in a stance of simulation. In the end, it is a duplicity that breeds duplicity.

Christian writers opposed the *duplicitas* of spectacle to the *simplicitas* of drama – another dispositive involving perception, desire, and action, but operating in reverse. *Simplicitas* is a perceptual stance that triggers affective processes and culminates in ways of seeing. As I have argued elsewhere (Bino 2025), the notion of *simplicitas* enters patristic exegesis already laden with Old- and New

Testament resonances. The simple corresponds to the Hebrew *tāmîm*: a whole, blameless person who listens to and practises God's word and is now able to see – indeed, to know – the Word revealed in Christ. *Haplous* – literally 'undivided' – is the key term in the Gospel saying about the 'sound' (or 'single') eye found in Matthew 6:22–23 and Luke 11:34. It names a gnoseologic and existential posture: a way of knowing and of being. The *haplous* person 'looks to God' with their whole being – heart, eye, word, and deed. For them, God, now accessible to every sense, becomes a living model that can be imitated. This unified, integral vision of the world is incompatible with the distance of spectacle and with the danger inherent in its duplicity. Tertullian (*De spectaculis* 2) calls it an intimate, inward vision – he uses the term *penitus*. It assumes an experiential point of view that arises 'from within' the drama of salvation: a drama whose *ratio* the individual has come to understand and in which they recognise themselves as a first-person participant, being a creature made in the image and likeness of God. This dramatic inclusion prevents them from adopting the stance of a spectator who looks on from the outside. Constantly an actor within the drama, the participant enacts their role without any split between *intus* and *foris*, between being and seeming; they are not trapped by appearances and will not be deceived by them. Though visible to others, they display themselves only before God – the sole participating spectator, whom Clement of Alexandria calls *synagonistès*, a co-actor (Lugaresi 2008: 406–417). Besides being 'inward', the simple gaze is also 'close-up' or, better, proximate. This means not only that the individual 'sees from nearby', but that they recognise their likeness to God and to other human beings – their very neighbours. Augustine explains that "it is not by spatial intervals that we approach God or distance ourselves from him. By your unlikeness to God you have gone far from him; as you become like him, you draw very near" (*Enarratio in Psalmum 99*, 5).

This awareness defines the responsibility of the gaze: what one sees depends entirely on the subject's intention in directing that gaze. Set as the foundation of all knowledge, this principle of responsibility leads to four consequences. First, it reorders desires and *affectus*: they no longer stop at what is merely visible or remain self-referential; instead, they reach beyond and become transitive. One loves the world not for how it appears, but because it is created; one loves human beings not for their appearance or possessions, but because they share the same ontological likeness. Second, it clarifies that humanity's role on the world's stage lies in being creatures similar-but-not-equal to the image of God revealed in Christ. Third, it makes clear that the aim of dramatic action is to recover the lost likeness by taking up the filial role of which Christ is the perfect model. Fourth, it shows that to enact the filial role, the human being must 'work on themselves', bringing eyes, words, and deeds into accord with their constitutive status as *imago Dei*. This 'doing as' is an imitation that harmonises and unifies *intus* and *foris*, *homo* and *habitus*, in opposition to simulation, which tears them apart. In short, the simple gaze generates unity.

Just as the spectacular dispositive unfolds in three visual processes, so the dramatic dispositive takes shape in three ways of seeing – three specifically Christian spectacles, each set in opposition to its pagan counterpart. Augustine states outright that the faithful must be offered spectacles in place of spectacles, almost as an antidote (*Enarratio in Psalmum 39*, 9). Thus, Christian spectacles replace their pagan counterparts in three ways: participatory contemplation of creation's beauty – offered in praise of the Creator – supplants the blind frenzy for the *vanitates* of the circus; the drama of salvation history, enacted in the theatre of the mind, displaces the simulated *fabulae* of the pagan boards; and acts of mercy towards suffering fellow-human beings in daily life take the place of the pleasure once drawn from the pain of the other in the arena. The conjunction of these three processes of vision constitutes the enactment of the dramatic strategy by which human beings orient their gaze towards reality in order to gain knowledge of the truth and ground their action upon it. For this reason, the three *spectacula christianorum* are intertwined and mutually interdependent.

However, everything begins with the participatory visualisation of the drama of salvation in the theatre of the mind. This is the only Christian spectacle that is dramaturgically structured, and it serves as the imaginative exercise that first re-orients the gaze *towards* the world and then shapes action *within* it.

1.3 The Theatre of the Mind: *Agere Memoriam*

The re-orienting force of imaginative representation is already present in Origen's idea of the heart's inner chamber (*tameion*) (Perrone 2006) and in Chrysostom's spiritual theatre (*pneumatikon theatron*) (Lugaresi 2008: 803–805). Augustine, however, remains the best guide to the theatre of the mind as an instrument for disciplining the gaze. His "psychology of human knowledge" – to use Gerard O'Daly's phrase (1987) – gave the Latin Middle Ages the theological framework for understanding the dynamics of interior perception, its relation to sense perception, and the soul's imaginative capacity.

However, *theatre of the mind* should not be taken to encompass Augustine's entire theory of interior vision, refined over more than thirty years of reflection. Instead, it refers specifically to the aspect concerned with a gaze converted and re-oriented by faith towards humanity's true wisdom, which is *cultus Dei*: namely recognising the ontological image of God in the human being and actively remembering it (*De Trinitate* 14:1). Indeed, Augustine employs the noun *theatrum* for the inner space of vision only when he means that the eye of the mind is focused on the *spectaculum spiritale* (*Sermo 373*, 5), the *spectaculum divinum* (*Enarratio in Psalmum 80*, 23), the *spectaculum verbi Dei* (*Enarratio in Psalmum 143*, 15). Within this context, Augustine distinguishes between the *theatrum cordis* (*Sermo 343*, 5), where the drama of salvation – or the deeds of the martyrs – are staged before the mind's eye, and the *theatrum conscientiae* (*Sermo 306E*, 2 and *154A*, 3), where the struggle unfolds between the mind that heeds the *lex* and the flesh that resists it.[2] In fact, Augustine is not speaking of two separate inner spaces but of a single locus – the *theatrum pectoris* of *Sermo 315*, 7:10 and *163B*, 5 – where two kinds of spectacle follow one another. God and the human being share the same stage, but in different roles. In the first spectacle the human being is a witness: they see, first-person, a scene in which God is the protagonist – or *editor* who sets it in motion. In the second spectacle, the human being is the performer: a charioteer, a tightrope-walker, the Pauline athlete who strives to align desires and *affectus* with right will. Here God plays the role of spectator, aiding the human and continually reminding them of what they saw in the first spectacle, which thus becomes the model for conduct.

The inner eye opens onto God's spectacles in two situations: when a person meditates on Scripture, and when they listen to its public reading – followed by the sermon – during the liturgy. Although these settings differ, they share two features. First, God's spectacles are utterly incompatible with *cupiditas spectaculorum*; to 'see' them, a person must willingly shut the doors of the senses to external stimuli and purge the eye of the soul of *curiositas*. Second, both circumstances initiate a process that actualises the 'memory of God' already present within the *mens* of the human being, created in His image and likeness.

Meditation is the technique – or rather, the art – by which memory constructs the presence of the divine (Carruthers 1998): entirely interior, it demands silence and recollection. As Gehl (1987: 131) notes, for Augustine *silentium* is not mere absence of sound but "the pregnant precondition" for the inward hearing of the Word and the vision of the *Verbum caro*. It is an all-encompassing withdrawal from worldly things, indispensable both to the study of the things of God and to the revelation of eternal wisdom (Leclercq 1961, Carruthers 2018, Henriet 2019). This is the active silence in which Ambrose reads (*Confessiones* 6:3:3), and the dialogic silence that absorbs Augustine and his mother at Ostia, where – cut off from the world – they glimpse, for a moment, the firstfruits of the Spirit. Such silence, Augustine says, generates a different sensory attention that

---

[2] It is the struggle against the *voluntas carnalis*, the root of the emotional rift in humankind after the primal rebellion discussed by Boquet and Nagy 2018: 25–27.

enables the perception of the divine, immersing the human being into an "inward joy":

> If, for anyone, the tumult of the flesh were hushed; if the phantasms of earth, water, and air lay still; if the very heavens themselves were veiled, and the soul itself were silent, transcending itself in ceasing even to reflect upon itself; if every dream and vision of the imagination were set aside, and every tongue, every sign, and all that passes away fell utterly mute – ... then, if they all were to fall silent, having turned our ears to Him who made them, He alone would speak, not through them but by Himself. And we should hear His word. ... Him whom we love in these things we should hear directly, without their mediation. Such was the moment when, stretching forth, we touched in one swift act of the mind the eternal Wisdom abiding beyond all things. Ah, if only it might endure, and all lesser visions, so immeasurably inferior, be withdrawn! Then that alone could ravish, absorb, and enfold with inward joys the one to whom such vision is granted. (*Confessiones* 9:10:25)

The idea that voluntary interior silence re-orients the senses appears again in *De Vera Religione* (49–51). Augustine links it to meditative reading of Scripture: only by choosing not to rest the mind's eyes on the *phantasmata* with which memory is imbued – and which screen the truth – can a person empty the inner theatre of everything that sends thought wandering (*vaga cogitatione*) and fill it with God's spectacles. By contrast, those 'salutary' spectacles refresh a soul troubled by *vana curiositas* and serve as a medicine that heals the inner eye, making it ever more capable of sight. This cyclical purification of the inner eye is continence, a cooperative work of both human being and God. It is not a rejection or elimination of visible and sensible objects, but rather "a collection of the soul's energy of attention and *affectus* which has been 'poured out' onto sensible objects" (Miles 1983: 133). Continence is, first, the human capacity to *colligere et redigere in unum* (*Confessiones* 10:29:40): a sensory recollection and re-ordering that restores the unity of *intus* and *foris*. It is also the grace of God that frees the inner person from the slavery of *concupiscentia*. Finally, continence is the *ostium* – the gate of the heart's mouth – that guards this restored unity (*De Continentia* 1–2) and turns it into the theatre of the interior spectacle.

To summarise: through the twin movement of emptying-silence and recollection-sensory introflexion – what Butler (1951: 29–31) aptly calls "introversion" – a person becomes present to themselves and simultaneously situates themselves in the very presence of the *spectaculum Verbi Dei*. That spectacle then serves as the *disciplina* – in Augustine's sense (*De Trinitate* 14:1) – by which the inner person learns to shape the outer person.

A different imaginative process unfolds when Scripture is heard in public assembly. In that setting, the listener must deliberately turn body and soul away from the tangible *voluptates theatrorum*. The eyes of the flesh must close to the *spectacula nugatoria et vana*, blocking the machinery of sensual desire and its after-effects; only then can the eyes of the mind open to the holy spectacles that set desire and emotion back in order. This interior reversal depends on a radical choice of place: the church rather than the theatre. It also rests on a radical choice of object: the truth of Scripture rather than the fiction of the *fabula*. From that initial renunciation, the composition of the vision begins – a process Augustine describes in several of his homiletic writings.[3]

First, the vision depends on the time in which it is produced. This is not merely what we would now call an 'occasion'. Augustine posits a strong link between ritual time and real time, grounded in memory's power to make the past present again, and he explains that link with the verb *repraesentare*. Thus, the anniversary of the martyrdom of Perpetua and Felicity "recalls the day to memory (*in memoriam revocat*) and, in a certain way, presents it anew (*et quodam modo repraesentat*) the day on which the saints ... gloriously attained eternal blessedness" (*Sermo 280*, 1); the celebration of Christ's Passion is a *recordatio* that "almost makes present (*quasi repraesentat*) what happened long ago and stirs us as though we saw the Lord hanging on the cross" (*Enarratio in Psalmum 21II*, 1); Easter, likewise, *commemorat* the Resurrection and "in some way brings that event again before our eyes (*quodammodo ... aspectibus repraesentat*)" (*Sermo 229D*, 2). Employing the verb *repraesentare* in all its polysemous shades – on which I shall return shortly – Augustine teaches that festal time *brings* the celebrated event *back into the now*, fixes it vividly in memory, and *presents it* before the eyes of the mind. On this 'return' of the event *in praesentia* rests the entire procedure of imaginative representation, which, in a homiletic context, unfolds in two stages. First comes the auditory, sensuous reception of the Scriptural reading, directly linked to the opening of the mental eye: "the sound is in the ears, the vision in the mind", Augustine observes (*Sermo 315*, 3:5). Second follows the participatory vision of the spectacle, of which the sermon is the form and the preacher the guide. The orator leads the hearer 'inside' the scene: he not only shows what is to be seen – constantly urging them to look, to attend, to compose a living, three-dimensional scene in motion – but also teaches them how to look, becoming virtually an emotional craftsman of mental images. Augustine himself describes this emotional interchange between preacher and audience. In his short handbook on teaching the faith (*De Catechizandis Rudibus* 15:23) he explains that

---

[3] Among the many occurrences, see, for example, *Sermo 4, 154A, 280, 313A,* and *315*.

words 'strike' the hearer – the verb is *afficere* – imprinting in the listener's soul the very face of the speaker's *affectus*. The preacher, in turn, is 'struck' by the listeners' response. This reciprocal co-action, rehearsed in the imagination, readies memory for its enactment in the ritual celebration, where the individuals share – truly and effectively – in the event now made present.

To summarise: the feast brings the event into time; the reading makes it audible to the faithful's outward senses and opens their inward senses; the sermon presents it before their minds as a spectacle that engages their *affectus*; the rite realises its presence.

Whether in meditation or in listening to Scripture, the composition of God's spectacle always turns on presence and is governed by memory. In her study of memory in Augustine, Cillerai (2008: 351–352) shows that memory is "the foundation ... of the very nature of the *homo interior* and of his relationship with God". What makes memory the 'venter' of the *mens* is its power to produce presence and make it perceptible: presence in time, presence in knowledge, and the self-presence that lets a person recognise themselves as *capax Dei*. This self-memory rests not on a Platonic theory of innate ideas but on an ontological affinity between mind and intelligible reality, between the human being made *ad imaginem et similitudinem* and God. By turning its cognitive tension from worldly things to truth, the individual 'makes memory of God': recognising Him as present in the very nature of the *mens* and actualising that memory. In other words, the individual transforms the memory of God from a 'constitutive presence' – ontologically given yet absent until acknowledged – into a 'living recollection'. Assisted by the grace of illumination and by Christ the mediator, "the road paved with humanity" (*De Trinitate* 4:1), this living memory enables the individual to return to the divine likeness. *Recordatio* and *commemoratio* are therefore an *agere memoriam*: making the human-God relationship present and participatory now, even though it will be fulfilled only at the end of time. Active memory gives that relationship experiential form.

The nexus between memory and presence is a cornerstone of Christianity that can rightly be called a religion of memory precisely because the actualising remembrance of God's act of salvation constitutes both the content of belief and the very object of worship. In his classic study of memory and *commemoratio* in the Middle Ages, Oexle (1976) notes that the Latin *memoria* carries two semantic layers. The first, corresponding to Greek *mneme*, is the faculty of recalling – bringing latent knowledge and experience back into the present. The second, matching Greek *anamnesis*, goes beyond recollection: it is a process that makes the past operatively present. Contemporary theological reflection on anamnestic processes likewise distinguishes between subjective memory (mere recollection) and objective memory (the memorial), the latter alone being able to render the past salvific act present without duplicating or repeating it (Mazza 2007).

This distinction between *mneme* and *anamnesis* is characteristic of medieval Christian thought, which always understood representation as a memorative and dramatic process – never as an analogical, mimetic reproduction. The revelation of a God who makes himself present in the world – Mondzain's apt "*carnation iconique*" (2003: 56) – undermines the Platonic-Aristotelian notion of representation, which here I take to mean a copy-like and defective reproduction (replica), as Palumbo (2008) details.[4] Notably, the sense of *repraesentare* as 'replicate/copy' is absent from patristic and medieval Latin lexica and does not occur in liturgical, exegetical, or homiletic sources until the early modern period (Bino 2021b).

Instead, three principal semantic foci can be isolated. The first refers to an intensification of presence proper to epiphanic showing: it denotes both the physical act of presenting something to the senses, and the mental visualisation of an object, understood as speculative 'apprehension'. The second refers to the iteration of presence: the 'bringing back' of something in space ('returning it') or in time ('reliving it'). The third invokes the logic of vicariousness: it covers both systems of personal delegation ('acting on someone's behalf') and figurative or symbolic modes of signification (Hofmann 1974, Ginzburg 1999: 97–119, Lagerlund 2007).

Rather, the polysemy of *repraesentare* concerns the modes of presence (physical, intellectual, symbolic) and the ways of producing it (strengthening, iteration, and vicariousness). When a human being *repraesentat* salvation-history, they are not reproducing an identical duplicate; instead, they enact its memory and 'make it present', presenting themselves on the stage where it unfolds. They make it present and make themselves present, both by meditating on Scripture in the theatre of the mind and by re-actualising it within the rites.

How that presence is produced and played out is what I explore in the two texts analysed here.

---

[4] See p. 11, footnote 7: "In the act of representation something is made present to the human subject without ceasing to remain separated from them by a distance that ... can never be abolished. Representation is an act in which the thing represented is reproduced and, in that reproduction, becomes accessible to visibility." Reproduction, however, never produces an identical copy; a distance and an absence always remain. Within that framework, the notion of the visible image as *mimema* becomes fully intelligible – an image that constitutes a deficient, fallible presence in relation to the ontological fullness of the absent object it aims at by imitating its presence.

1.4 Avatar: Production of Presence

In light of the dramatic dispositive of vision and the memorial sense of representation, it should now be apparent why I chose the term *avatar* to name the imaginal body the devotee fashions in order to be present within the memorial play. Even so, a few further clarifications are needed, chiefly of a semantic nature.

The contexts in which the term avatar is used are mostly two.

The first is its original setting. In Sanskrit, *avatāra* (Latin *descensus*) comes from the verb *avatṛ*, meaning "to descend into/from". In Hindu tradition it denotes a deity – most often Viṣṇu – who descends among human beings in a visible form to restore cosmic order and guide humankind. Because Hindu cosmology is cyclical, avatars recur, and each one is a (frequently partial and non-human) manifestation suited to a specific moment. When its task is complete, the *avatāra* dissolves or is re-absorbed into the god (Kinsley 1987: 14–15). Comparative theologians who study the deity's descent as avatar in the various Hindu traditions and set it beside the Christian Incarnation of the Word come to the same conclusion (Parrinder 1997, Sheth 2002, Michael 2016). To them, both phenomena are forms of presence – what Gumbrecht (2004) calls "productions of presence": their outcome is the tangibility proper to what is material. The *avatāra*, however, is a theophany. It is neither the god in full ontological presence nor a mere appearance; rather, it is a descent – which entails a rupture – that is both ahistorical and recurrent, assuming a concrete, earthly form that makes the divine perceptible, albeit only for a time. Christ, by contrast, is God's revelation: the personal union of divine and human natures; he is *Verbum caro*, and not simply Word in flesh. The Word (the Son) is consubstantial with the Father, the co-essential image of God. His coming is God's birth into human existence – within the mutable dimensions of space and time – and entails *kenōsis*, the self-emptying of the atemporal, immutable mode. The Incarnation is therefore a once-for-all historical event, permanent in its effect (through the Resurrection, human nature is configured to God's and abides in that state – see Braumann 1976).

In this first context, an avatar is a *form* of the subject's *presence*; what varies is how that presence is produced and its very type – merely apparent or enduring.

The second context is contemporary immersive media within the wider field of audiovisual technologies, where avatar refers to "graphical representations functioning as digital proxies through which the users of the internet, of a cyber-community or a computer–based interface . . . interact with synthetic objects or other avatars in the virtual world" (Pinotti 2020: 33). The avatar's required link to the real subject, together with its wide formal range – "ranging from simple drawings or photographic (self–)portraits to elaborate figures produced by CGI" (Pinotti 2023: 190) – means that an avatar is not merely a reproduction; it is also "a powerful identity-operator that allows for an infinite number of negotiations of selfhood" (Pinotti 2020: 33). The negotiation of a subject's identity through avatars in immersive fictional environments has long been at the centre of interdisciplinary debate (mediological, philosophical, psychological, and neuroscientific) which has examined its mechanisms and emotive-sensory effects using various methodological approaches. In this field, too, the category of *presence* plays a fundamental hermeneutic role and is interwoven with that of *point of view*. Particularly, scholars note that avatars correspond to different models of subject presence. They do this by manipulating two aspects of experience: the spatial dimension – the feeling of 'being there' – and the temporal dimension, which is tied to the perception of action and movement (Eugeni 2018). The experience of inhabiting a virtual space–time that is nevertheless fully sensory and emotional varies with what Pinotti (2020: 39) calls the "avatarisation of the gaze" – that is, the extent to which the subject's viewpoint overlaps with that of the avatar. In other words, it changes depending on how closely the user's own point of view aligns with that of the avatar. It reaches its highest degree when the subject maintains "the visual and aural position" of the avatar, which Eugeni (2012: 25) has defined as the "first person shot": "a figure which expresses in sensorial terms ... the idea of subject and subjective identity. ... It represents the sight of located, embodied, enworlded, active, dynamic, and hybrid agents ..., and consequently, its perceptual, practical, emotional, living and ongoing experience".

In this second context, an avatar is always a fictional stand-in for its real–world user, bound to that user by an identity link. Yet the *modes of representation* shift, producing a semantic and functional short-circuit between the duplicative reproduction of the subject (the avatar as double) and the complex, experiential production of a sensation of presence.

The way I use the term avatar borrows something from both earlier contexts: the first, concerned with *forms of presence*, and the second, with *modes of representation*. However, the differing semantics of representation, the Christian dramatic dispositive of vision, and the 'immersive' effects this dispositive exerts on medieval narrative and figurative forms – emphasised by Bleumer (2012) – together reshape the mechanisms of presence and participation inherent in imaginative experience.

Against this backdrop, I define the avatar as a 'postural figure' that enables the subject to re-locate their perceptual and emotional faculties and thus make themselves present inside the imaginal environment they construct. The avatar is not the subject's double; rather, it is a reconfiguration of the subject's psychosomatic unity (in Bynum's sense of persona, 1995: 157–199). This reconfiguration allows the subject themself to perceive, in a fully personal way, a form of experience that is distinct from ordinary material reality. Four stages lead to this postural configuration of the avatar, which I outline next.

First, the discipline of the physical body: through a series of material operations (silence / closure / emotional and sensory isolation; the ordering of space and time and their qualities; specific postures and gestures, and so on), the physical body prepares the construction of the imaginal environment.

Second, the formation of an inner gaze (by gaze I mean perception) through *intentio* understood as the "creative tension" that embraces "concentration, 'intensity' of memory, intellect, and ... emotional attitude" (Carruthers 1998: 15). *Intentio* does not shift the viewpoint – it remains the subject's own, in the first person – but it does change the orientation of the gaze (*where* one looks) and its affective colouring (*how* one looks). In other words, *intentio* names both the 'direction' of the eye and its 'disposition': a posture of the gaze that guides vision and gives it an emotional perspective.

Third, the introflected and affectively positioned gaze produces the presence of the imaginal environment and furnishes it with a diegetic framework, according to a 'dramatic and perspectival schema' that determines its form, movement, and emotional impact. It achieves this by using memory as a "compositional art" (Carruthers 1998: 9) and by drawing on what Kiening (2019: 59) calls "media forms", meaning "all those things [texts, sermons, objects, images, liturgical-ritual actions etc.] that can be brought into view for the senses or the imagination" and create the impression "that one is present to the events oneself".

Fourth, the subject re-locates themself inside the dramatic environment, producing their presence as a 'character in the drama'; in theatrical terms, they step onstage and assume a specific role. Since the drama displays memorative characteristics, the subject's re-location follows the re-presentational logic of memory rather than the duplicative logics that set the spatio-temporal dimension of reality against that of fiction. In this process, the subject enters a 'present' and becomes the agent of their own being-there in time and space, actively constructing and manipulating both spatial and temporal dimensions of representation. The role the subject enacts in the memorial play can vary. It may coincide with the role they have chosen in ordinary life, or it may merge with that of particular character in the drama. In the first case, the subject projects their personal identity into the play and adopts the postural figure that matches their own model or *habitus* of life. In the second, they quite literally step into another's shoes, adopting that character's viewpoint, actions, gestures, sensations, and emotions. In both scenarios the avatar generated reinforces the subject's personal presence: it gives interior posture a concrete, physio-sensory form and turns it into lived experience.

To sum up: the first two stages deal with the sensory-emotional introversion that prepares the vision, while the third and fourth are re-presentational processes, shaping the vision's dramaturgy and the part the subject plays within it. Both instances are, in effect, productions of presence.

1.5 Dramaturgies of Presence

Viewed through the re-presentational processes just outlined, the two texts I examine disclose two distinct *dramaturgies of presence*: one meditative and inward, the other ritual and outward. In each case the devotee engages in their dramatic relationship with God. What makes them especially valuable for the history of the senses and emotions is that, in both cases, this relationship unfolds within the drama of Christ's life and reaches its climax in the Passion scene. Whatever happens to Christ, and whatever he feels, is seen and lived by the devotee according to different postures that are mutually bound to the way the scene itself is constructed, that is, its underlying dramaturgical schema.

Thanks largely to the work of Chazelle (2001) and Fulton Brown (2002), it is now well established that the ways in which the Passion was conceived, narrated, and 'set in images' changed over the centuries in step with the growing significance that Christ's flesh acquired in contemporary Christological, soteriological and anthropological reflection. From the Carolingian era to the eleventh century, Christ's true humanity was crucial to the three great debates on images, divine predestination, and Eucharistic realism. During that period, the representation of the Passion came to function as a 'discipline of the gaze': it taught the devotee to see the suffering body of Jesus on the cross as if present (*quasi praesentialiter*) and close at hand. Narrative, exegetical and euchological texts, together with rites and figurative art, offered a dramatic image of the Crucified's wounded body, training the believer's eyes to manage that powerful 'sense of presence', to form an engaged relationship with that body and to feel an appropriate emotional response. By contrast, between the twelfth and fourteenth centuries, the radical transformation of Passion imagery must be read against a different backdrop: the growing importance of the senses and emotions for defining the individual, the rising prominence of the laity, the explosion of the mendicant orders and the flowering of Eucharistic devotion. Moreover, a strong 'sense of history' and what Hardison (1965: 43) termed a "search for reality" led to an expansion of the Passion narrative, transforming it into a drama articulated in scenes, each composed of minutely rendered actions.

The 'in-presence' relationship between believer and God shifted progressively onto the plane of concrete sensual perception and of active participation in the whole Passion event. The believer's involvement unfolded in stages. At first, one merely *learned to see* Christ's pain. Seeing grew into *sharing* that suffering. Sharing deepened into *identifying* with the one who felt it. *Identification*, in turn, led to *conforming*: the devotee became, in the first person, suffering flesh and grieving heart. In this way an inward sense of presence was transformed into bodily sensation and concrete action, a shift that ultimately generated dramatic re-presentations of the Passion, public and community-related (Bino 2008).

The texts I have chosen clearly illustrate this second shift, from seeing to acting, from sharing to conforming, because each one offers a different representational scheme that matches the posture the devotee adopts to build the scene, inhabit it, and perform a role within it. Three postures recur most often.

The first posture is affective participation. The devotee's gaze is situated 'inside' a relationship that shapes how the scene is framed: what is represented is not what happens to Christ, nor his actions, but the sensations and emotions experienced by someone with whom one has an affective bond. This is not a generic 'affective piety'. Rather, it refers to *affectus* as a "form of representation", a notion – clarified by Lia (2007) – that is distinctive of Cistercian theology, and in particular of Bernard of Clairvaux's theological aesthetics. Etymologically, *affectus* is the past participle of *afficere*. In the passive, *affici* means 'to be touched', 'impressed', and therefore 'altered' or 'drawn'. Hence, *affectus* names both God's action, imprinting His image on humanity at creation, and human longing for that image. It is, in short, the 'loving relationship' between God and humankind: the reciprocity that bound them before the Fall, and the bond re-established by the Incarnation and Passion of Christ. In the latter case, *affectus* denotes God's restorative love, whereby, by making Himself similar to humanity, He reaches the depths of its dissimilarity and offers the possibility of returning to the image. As a form of representation, *affectus* unfolds in fraternal and friendly bonds but, above all, in spousal love – centred on Mary Magdalene – and maternal love, which makes the Virgin's affection the dramaturgical key to Christ's life. Within the Passion narrative, the complementary meanings of Magdalene's tears and Mary's tears gave rise to traditions of the *lamentation* and *compassion* through which the interplay of affective roles enacted by those who took part in that event could be 'staged'.

The second posture is mimetic identification. Here the devotee's gaze moves from *within* an affective bond to standing *with* the figure to whom that bond is directed. The scene is now watched from inside the action: the devotee lives each event *alongside* the protagonist, copying their gestures and sharing their feelings and sensations in a psychagogic process of identification. The viewpoint is not fully first-person; rather, the gap between observer and observed collapses into a single, aligned subjectivity. This change of perspective is decisive. It inserts an 'as' into the act of representation and activates a principle of 'fiction' that is not simulation but, in Bettetini's (2004) terms, a "figure of truth": the self is moulded by imitating the other until identification is achieved.

Franciscan spirituality adopted this posture and pushed it to the limit. As a concrete enactment of the Gospel in living flesh, the *sequela Christi* was not merely a 'doing as' Christ does but a 'becoming like' him, namely a reshaping of the self until full conformity is reached. This embodiment of the loving relationship with God leads to a third posture: complete identification. Here the devotee goes beyond projecting themselves into the scene, seeing Christ's presence in a sensual way, beyond forming an affective bond, beyond imitating Christ's actions and sharing his emotions. They identify with him so completely that their natural body – and every sense – becomes a Christic body. This new perspective opens up two participatory levels of the Lord's life, especially in relation to his Passion. On the social, chiefly lay level, devotional practices aimed to reshape human relationships through Passion piety, treating Christ's suffering as the paradigm of concrete charity; from this impulse emerged the so-called 'theatre of mercy', expressed above all in confraternal rites. On the personal and mystical level, devotees pursued an intimate imitation and a full physical-mental-ethical conformity to Christ. From this sphere arose what Bartolomei Romagnoli (2021) calls the "drama of sacrificial identification": a continual interweaving of presence-vision (*contemplatio*), affective participation (*compartecipatio*), and mimetic identification (*conformatio*).

The following sections investigate how these postures function within the two dramaturgies of presence and what re-presentational and psychosomatic effects they produce.

2 Projecting Presence: 'Becoming' Magdalene

Aelred of Rievaulx's *De institutione inclusarum* (1160–1162), written for his anchoress sister, presents – in linear fashion – the process of physical-perceptual closure from an outside and sensory-affective opening within an inside, which enables the configuration of the avatar and the formation of visionary experience.[5] The work is structured in three sections, and Aelred himself outlines the content of each one.[6]

---

[5] References are to Macpherson's 1971 English translation, cited by page (hereafter *R.R.*); Latin citations are to Talbot's 1971 edition, cited by line (hereafter *Inst. Incl.*).
[6] On the composition of the work, see Dutton 1983 and Maude 2021.

The first part lays down the "institutions for bodily observances by which a recluse may govern the behaviour of the outward man" (*R.R.*: 102): it describes the complex of operations by which the subject disciplines the physical body and turns the senses inward. The second offers "directions for cleansing the inner man from vices and adorning him with virtues" (*R.R.*: 102): it concerns the affective configuration of the inner gaze and the preparation of the theatre of the mind. The third, finally, is "a threefold meditation to enable you to stir up the love of God in yourself, feed it and keep it burning" (*R.R.*: 102): it corresponds to the production of presence of the memorial play by the subject and the avatar through which they act.

The work's representational scheme is explicitly oriented towards a posture of affective co-participation. Yet two factors must guide the analysis of its process: first, the twofold dynamic of exterior-interior, closure-openness is played entirely within the already enclosed interior of the cell; second, the subject is a woman, living alone and withdrawn from the world.[7] If withdrawal from external reality is thus presupposed, the maintenance of closure must be continually 'kept under surveillance' so as to accord with the individual's specific status. Hence, the detailed regulatory system is twofold: securing the cell's status as a wholly interior environment; and ensuring that the subject adopts a sensory-affective posture enabling the reconfiguration of a new psychosomatic identity within that interior. It is from the organisation of this normative system that the analysis must begin.

2.1 The *Regula*: Economy of Presence

In the prologue, Aelred briefly states what his book is (*Inst. Incl.*: 1–16). It is not a schematic formulary of practices (*formula certa*) devised to direct the private manner of life his sister has embraced for Christ. Rather, it is a founded rule (*certa regula*) that will not guide her alone in bringing into harmony (*ad componendum*) the condition of the outward man with her vocation, but will also serve other women who choose a similar life (*Inst. Incl.*: 176–79).[8] As he had stressed in the *Speculum Charitatis* (3, 35), every rule has its own specific way of 'ordering' the life of those who voluntarily renounce the world and offer themselves to God. The rule not only gathers the exercises required of body and

---

[7] The literature on female reclusion is now extensive; see, at a minimum, Herbert McAvoy 2011, and the essay collections Herbert McAvoy and Hughes-Edwards 2005 and Gunn and Herbert McAvoy 2017.

[8] I take Aelred's contrast between *formula certa* and *certa regula* to be anything but casual; it gestures, rather elegantly, towards a more fully institutional definition of reclusion. The rule is *certa*, because it rests on various *instituta* of the Fathers and gives a firmer foundation to reclusion as a choice not of one individual but of many. For the broader institutional framing of medieval religious life, see Melville 2025.

spirit; it 'manages' them, modifies how the practices are to be observed and distributed over time, how spaces are to be organised, and how interpersonal relations are to be conducted. This internal 'economy' forms the identity-bearing armature of any rule: it must be known, weighed, and observed by anyone who undertakes it, for it will shape a determinate *habitus vivendi* and an equally determinate affective relation to God.

Both Aelred and his sister chose a life withdrawn from the world and dedicated to God. Yet, the two choices differ markedly. As L'Hermite-Leclercq (1999) underscores, Aelred is fully aware of this difference and builds his treatise upon it. He knows himself to belong to a community-body of which every monk is a member: the Cistercian rule he embraced orders the physical and spiritual practices that regulate spaces, times, actions, and speech within a single 'relational unit'. Its aim is to shape a collective identity – a group conscious of sharing a pattern of behaviour (Bynum 1982: 102–106). He also knows that his is a horizontal community, grounded in the voluntary and unanimous adherence of many to charity (Cariboni 2011), or – in Rosenwein's terms (2006) – an "emotional community". Aelred translates the ideal of charity into a precise "communal affective model" (Boquet 2005: 275), namely spiritual friendship, which he crystallises in the image of the familial affection between Jesus and the disciple John with which he concludes the *Speculum Charitatis* (3:110).

The sister's choice, by contrast, is an isolated, solitary life *intra cellulam*, an enclosed space with the exit barred (*obstruso exitu*). On entering it she performs three acts: she renounces the world; she hides herself from the world, desiring not to be seen (*non videri*); she dies to the world and is buried with Christ (*Inst. Incl.*: 439–442). This burial – as Jones (2012) shows in his study of the English rites of enclosure – is less a death than an initiation into a new life. The anchoress's isolation is thus a spatio-temporal shift of presence: she is absent from the world's stage and no longer keeps the time of its performance. Her solitude is a 'being with Christ alone'; all other relations are excluded. Therefore, the rule Aelred writes has to administer this form of presence according to the spatial and temporal order of the 'interior', disciplining a single psychosomatic identity and directing it to the one relationship with Christ. The sensory and affective dynamics it governs aim not at charity 'tasted' in the communal affect of the monastic *familia*, but at the exclusive love of two lovers. The model is spousal love, epitomised by the restful, delicious embrace of Magdalene at the feet of the risen Christ, the goal of the first of Aelred's three concluding meditations (*Inst. Incl.*: 1235–1237).

If a spousal relationship is the rule's telos, the rule must first discipline the cell, making it a space that ensures the outside's absence. In doing so, it produces a double presence of her alive, yet dead to the world, and him, present and living "to the end of the world" (Matthew 28: 20).

2.2 The Cell as Body: The Discipline of Presence

Aelred begins the rule by constructing the cell. He does so in two stages: a *pars destruens*, explaining how the cell is *not* to be inhabited (*Inst. Incl.*: 16–122), and a *pars construens*, shaping the posture of the outward man through a strict discipline of silence and time, by which he orders all activities and all relations (*Inst. Incl.*: 128–438). In both instances, he assimilates the cell to a body and uses this rhetorical figure – typical of the monastic tradition – to describe how material reality is perceived and its psychosomatic effects on the individual. In the pars *destruens*, the cell is an 'unprotected body' that loses its unity with the soul, which is exposed to the world's unruly sensuality. By contrast, in the pars *construens*, the cell is a 'guarded body' that keeps its oneness with the soul.

Aelred sets in opposition disorder and perceptual–emotional order, a contrast to be read against the background of his anthropology of the affections, effectively studied by Boquet (2005). In this case, however, he describes the process of perfect affective ordering that leads the individual to mystical union with God – a process he had already outlined in *Sermon 32* for the Feast of the Purification of Mary (Boquet 2017: 184–189). The person, he explains, is like a palace in which the *mens rationalis* is the sentry: it guards the body-as-building and keeps watch by day over *voluptas* and *vanitas* and by night over the vices. The bodily senses are the doors that open onto the exterior atrium (*memoria*), through which evil (*cupiditas*, articulated in the three desires for knowledge, wealth, and carnal pleasure) can enter, as well as good things (*caritas*). Through the door of thought (*cogitatio*), they pass into the interior atrium of the inner man (delight) and immediately enter the vestibule, where the will sits in judgment, choosing what to admit to the *domus* of consent. There the person feeds on its desires. Mystical union occurs when one keeps vigilant guard over the senses (the accesses to the palace's exterior atrium) so that memory is wholly occupied by the Lord, who passes through the body-as-building and inhabits it. When consent is joined by the affect of love and the delight of the spirit, everything passes into the most precious part of the person (the nuptial chamber), where the most intimate embrace takes place.

In our context, Aelred seems to invert the similitude – no longer the body as a building, but the cell as a body – and he describes the process of affective disorder. The *pars destruens* begins with an image of a split between the recluse's body and soul: her *membra* are shut within the cell's walls, yet the *mens* fails to keep watch; instead, it wanders aimlessly, splinters into worldly interests and anxieties, and is stirred by impure desires.[9] This split generates a sensory and affective tension *towards the world*, contrary to the cell's function. Aelred renders it through the image of the woman perpetually seated at the cell window, which has become almost her ear and mouth. The recluse listens and speaks: her sense-windows open, letting in *voluptas*, which then spreads through the rest of her limbs. When she, alone again, reflects (*cogitat*) on what she has heard, everything returns in the form of an image before the eyes of the heart. The interior vision rebounds onto her senses and dulls them (the tongue stammers, sight grows dim, the body sways), preventing her from devoting herself to the memory of God. Aelred repeats the point several times: to sit at the window is to leave the cell and let the world in with its three lusts. The cell/body is transformed: from a place of closure and intactness, it becomes a market, a school, a hospice, and – its access flung wide (*dilatato foramine*) – even a brothel through which one goes in and out.

It is therefore necessary to guard the cell's entrances and keep vigil over anyone who approaches. Guarding and protecting are the key words of the *pars construens*, which seeks to restore within the cell the shattered body-soul unity through a discipline of presence articulated in three actions: exclusion, perceptual-emotional introflection, and temporal ordering. First, the senses/door-windows are kept under guard to ensure that the world remains shut outside. Yet because what is exterior can enter through interpersonal relations, these relations are regulated so that every affective motion *ad extra* is contained or eliminated. Hearing and active sight are moderated because they generate inner images that occupy memory; touch and passive sight (*the way one shows oneself* through posture and clothing) are sources of vice and are almost entirely eliminated. Second, silence becomes the body's stable condition (*sede et tace*), required for the inner peace of the soul. Lest that peace be disturbed, exterior speech is disciplined, establishing when to speak, about what, with whom, and in what manner. Third, the strictest bodily needs (meals, sleep), work, and – above all – interior speech (reading, prayer, meditation) are distributed according to a detailed temporal order, daily and yearly. The daily order follows the liturgical rhythm of the canonical hours (nocturn, matins, prime, terce, sext, none, vespers, and compline). The yearly order overlays the cycle of the seasons onto ritual time and is divided into two blocks: from the Feast of the Exaltation of the Cross to Lent, and from Easter

---

[9] The three distractions of the soul are the three forms of *cupiditas*. Contrary to Boquet (2005: 260–262), I do not take *pervagatio* to be a specifically feminine feature. In Aelred, *pervagatio cordis/mentis* is equivalent to *spiritualis vagatio*, that is, to *curiositas* (see Sermo 43, *In nativitate sancti Ioannis Baptistae*: 27, where he sets out its features, which overlap with those in the *Inst. Incl.*: 16–34).

to the Exaltation of the Cross. At the centre stands Lent, the privileged time of purification that prescribes a regime of total silence and of fasting of the senses and from activity, which facilitates delving into Scripture, a realignment of the inner movements of the heart, and the affective tension towards God (Dietz 2022). Lent is the emblematic symbol of the fast from the world: it becomes the exemplary time of the cell and, at the same time, the season in which the recluse desires her Lord even more. Lent is her "wedding day" (*R.R.*: 59).

The establishment of this precise temporal order marks a pivotal moment in Aelred's discipline of the cell/body. Christian time is a ferial *continuum* punctuated by festal events – a state of perpetual mnemonic tension that allows the person to bridge the gap between the finite dimension of the human being and the infinite dimension of God, made accessible through the remembrance of Christ's incarnation, passion, and resurrection (Alzati 2005). *Commemoratio* 'brings back' the mystery of salvation from past and future into the *hodie* of the present, allowing one to experience it: as for Augustine, so for Aelred representation is a mnemonic process understood as the strengthening and reiteration of presence.[10] Entering a ritual order of time is therefore a necessary condition for the mechanisms of production of presence.

In sum, the discipline of the cell recomposes the recluse's psychosomatic unity *within* the body and, through solitude and silence, produces her presence in a different spatio-temporal dimension. Yet, it shapes only the exterior posture of the one who chooses reclusion, limiting itself to producing a mere 'being in the presence of Christ': "she must sit alone ... believing that when alone she is never alone, for then she is with Christ" (*R.R.* 50). For this presence to become active – "listening to Christ and speaking with him" (*R.R.*: 51) – the woman must assume an appropriate inner affective configuration. That is the task of the rule's second section.

2.3 The Body as Vessel: Affective Posture

At the outset of the chapters devoted to ordering the inner man, Aelred urges the anchoress to redirect her gaze, to fix it on her soul, and to centre her attention there. *Cogitare* is the foundational act on which the rule's second section is built: it is the work of the *mens* which, having gathered and introflected all the senses, thinks and re-thinks (*revolvet*) its own condition and how to give that condition a form suited to a relationship of love with God. The norms that follow are thus 'spiritual exercises' meant to discipline the anchoress's psychosomatic unity *within* the soul, and to orient it towards the *dilectio Dei*. Body,

---

[10] For Aelred's use of the verb *repraesentare* together with the phrase *ad memoriam revocare*, see Bino 2021b.

senses, and desires are reread in this light. The body becomes a delicate container – a sensual earthen vessel that guards the woman's virginity, the precious and fragrant treasure the Lord longs for like a lover. Silent solitude, by contrast, becomes the fast from the world of one who has freely pledged herself to God (*Inst. Incl.*: 443–470).

Aelred distributes the spiritual practices in a lengthy allegorical narrative, punctuated by *exempla* and built around two parallel figures corresponding to two actions: first, stripping the recluse's soul of the pride of the old self, which keeps her far from God; second, clothing it fully with the humility of the new self, which draws her back to God. Both figures/actions are guided *by*, and oriented *towards*, charity – the driving force and goal of the whole process of discipline.[11] The first figure gathers the exercises of penance and contrition through which the woman trains her introflected senses, freeing them from the feeling of the flesh.[12] The instruments of this re-educative purification are, on the one hand, *continentia* which – in Augustine too – holds together *carnis afflictio* and divine grace; on the other, the *meditatio* of Scripture, which, like a mirror, illumines the interior senses, exposes *voluptas* and *curiositas*, and removes them (*Inst. Incl.*: 504–696). Through this interior 'training' the anchoress assumes the humble posture of the penitent who, by tradition, keeps her face lowered and eyes downcast, lies prostrate at Christ's feet, and 'pierces her heart', invoking his name and imploring forgiveness amid tears (Nagy 2000: 276–313, Bino 2021a). The second figure arranges the practices of virtue, which Aelred likens to the weft the soul weaves upon the warp of its humility, thereby fashioning the garment in which it will appear at the wedding with Christ. The exercise of virtue effects a change in the anchoress's affective posture: from humble penitent she becomes lover and bride (*Inst. Incl.*: 697–715).

The two figures/actions find their fulfilment in the concrete practice of charity, articulated as love of neighbour and love of God – allegorically, the threads with which the woman trims the hem of her wedding garment. Aelred, however, explains to the recluse that, by dying to the world, she has withdrawn from the active duty of loving others so as to devote herself solely to the love of God (*Inst. Incl.*: 773–872). Indeed, she has chosen to play a specific role: "recognise the state in which you are . . . . There were two sisters, Martha and

---

[11] This is the process outlined in *Speculum Charitatis* 1:24–27. Only charity makes human renewal possible, for it re-orients the soul's love towards the purpose for which it was created. In so doing, the psychosomatic unity of the human being is re-formed according to its status as the image of God. On this theme, see Boquet 2005: 161–165.

[12] Here Aelred employs the term *caro* to denote the bondage of the old self – *cupiditas* – whose remnants still linger within the *mens*. See *SC* 1: 27.

Mary. The one was busy, the other ... simply sat at Jesus' feet and listened to what he had to say. This is your role" (*R.R.*: 75).

As Aelred explains, the anchoress must play her part in two distinct ways, for "there are two elements in the love of God (*dilectio Dei*): interior dispositions (*affectus mentis*) and the performance of works (*effectus operis*). The latter lies in the practice of the virtues ..., a matter of a rule of life ... whereas the affections are nourished by wholesome meditation" (*R.R.*: 79). The rule therefore schools in *dilectio Dei*, which is at once the *effectus* of her practices and the emotional attitude – her *affectus* – to which she attains. Yet the discipline of the cell provides only the affective posture; it does not in itself effect the nuptial union of love. Only *meditatio* enables the soul to place itself actively in the presence of God: it is, as Boquet calls it (2005: 184), an "ascetic and mystical itinerary" through which memory produces a lived presence of God that approaches the threshold of 'real presence' and sacramental efficacy (Nouzille 2011). For Aelred, who repeatedly emphasises the tangible accessibility of Jesus's "sacred humanity" (Dutton 1992: 212), meditation generates the presence of an *affective and psychosomatic relationship* between the human person and God-made-flesh, allowing an experience of that relationship that is spiritual, but above all dynamic and sensory.

In sum, the rule has taught the recluse her part. First, it disciplined her exterior attitude, schooling her to 'stand only in the presence' of Christ. Then it 'clothed' her interior attitude, training her to be humble at his feet and attentive to his words. The accord between the two attitudes shaped by the cell (the fast of the senses and the desiring tension towards God) forms the affective posture of the bride who "yearns with all her ardour for Christ's embrace" (*R.R.*: 59).[13] Through meditation, the woman opens the interior theatre and gives form to the memorial play.

2.4 Time, Place, and Posture of Meditation

The onset of meditation is shaped by temporal circumstances (when the anchoress meditates), environmental contingencies (where she meditates), and the physical setting (how she meditates).

We have already seen that the cell corresponds to a dimension of ritual time and to a state of physical-sensorial closure that together produce a new form of subject's presence, absent to the world and yet affectively positioned. The relation between meditation and ritual time turns on the memory's

---

[13] Although Aelred offers the recluse a threefold meditation on the past, the present, and the future, *recordatio* operates only in the first, whose focus is the earthly life of Christ. This is the sole meditation that adopts the dramatic structure of the memorial play.

representational power; the relation between meditation and the space of the cell is a further 'entry into an interior'; finally, the relation between meditative posture and affective posture issues in the production of a 'postural figure', the avatar with which the subject renders herself present in the memorial play. Let us consider each point in turn.

Aelred states that *meditatio Verbi Dei* is a purifying, educative instrument that must occupy the anchoress's thought at every canonical hour (*Inst. Incl.*: 609–612). During Lent – the fast of the senses that prepares for the divine vision – meditation is prescribed even between Nocturns and Lauds (*Inst. Incl.*: 381–382), a vigil that recalls the watch at Christ's tomb while awaiting the rising of the lamb-bridegroom (Alzati 2005: 20). Thus, on the one hand, meditation is woven into ritual time – the canonical *hours* – which structures daily life in the cell according to the memory of the mystery of salvation realised in Christ: it enables the recluse to remain in constant relation with the divine, thereby disciplining her psychosomatic identity. On the other hand, meditation is a mnemonic instrument that amplifies the representational dimension of Lenten time, allowing the recluse to celebrate her nuptials with the Lord. In both cases, meditation acts as a mnemonic *medium* that actualises the presence summoned by ritual time.

The *locus* of meditation is the oratory, the only space described in the rule. A site of perpetual prayer, it stands as the condensed icon of the cell. It contains a single furnishing: an altar covered with a cloth of pure white linen. Upon the altar stands the lone crucifix, perhaps flanked by images of the Mother and of John. No other ornament is permitted. Aelred depicts the oratory solely by narrating the severe process by which the linen that swathes the altar is wrought; its final whiteness is a metaphor for the interior purity painfully won by the recluse (*Inst. Incl.*: 716–766). In a movement of progressive penetration into an interior, the cell is thus transformed into an oratory, and the oratory becomes the woman's *inner place*.

The transformation of the oratory into an inner place presupposes concord between *intus* and *foris*, between the soul's quiet and the cell's silence, between a mind cleared of every vain spectacle and an environment stripped of ornament (*Inst. Incl.*: 746–752). The woman's affective posture – humble lover at the Lord's feet – accords with the bodily posture she adopts for prayer, kneeling at the foot of the crucifix. The crucifix, once an image contemplated with the eyes of the body, becomes a *relational presence*: when she prays, she speaks to him, when she reads, she listens to him, when she meditates, she meets him. The anchoress sets the mnemonic process in motion by literally turning her now–cleansed inner eyes towards the past (*oculos defaecatos retorque ad posteriora*;

Inst. Incl.: 889–890). In so doing, she re-locates her personal presence within the scene recalled and projects into it her postural figure (her avatar).

2.5 'Becoming Magdalene' within the Memorial Play

Aelred parcels the remembrance of the past into a narrative of Jesus's earthly life divided into episodes. He gives this narrative scheme a locative, temporal, and dramatic shape: he arranges the events along an itinerary from place to place and from moment to moment, re-presenting them as they unfold. The result is a three-act drama, each act comprising six scenes, plus an epilogue.[14]

The anchoress is not a spectator outside the story but an actor within the drama, entrusted with the role of Christ's lover. In mnemotechnical terms, Aelred is a "master builder" – to borrow Carruthers's words (1993) – who stages a memory theatre designed as a spatio-temporal map. The recluse is the invited subject (the text bristles with imperatives and exhortations) who must activate that map with a specific affective colouring, thereby producing and performing the memorial play.

This process involves two operations: first, the relocation of the recluse's presence onto the (a)temporal plane of memory; second, the construction of the scenes from an affectively positioned point of view. This re-location of presence does not occur through a proxy or double that mediates between the woman's psychosomatic identity and the mnemonic experience. Instead, the anchoress projects her postural figure – namely, the sensory and emotional capacities disciplined within the cell – into the past that memory brings into the present. Thus, her avatar is a *first-person presence in a re-presented past*. Aelred conveys the punctual, aoristic coexistence of temporal planes by alternating past and present verbs: the woman sees now what happened then and, through memory, hears, acts, and feels in the present of that past. Memory scenes are always built from this first-person presence. Yet, as she moves within the spatio-temporal map of memory, the point of view continually shifts, each time generating a fresh affective perspective that reframes the scene in different ways. In return, the scenographic frame fashioned by her gaze acts upon the avatar, eliciting a physico-emotional response that determines *how the scene is played*. As an example, I present Aelred's composition of the Last Supper, emblematic both for its use of tenses and for the (physical and affective) positioning of the viewpoint together with the avatar's ensuing entry into action.

---

[14] The first act spans Jesus's childhood and adolescence, from the incarnation to the baptism; the third centres on the passion and resurrection. The middle act is devoted to mercy and juxtaposes three scenes of petition for forgiveness (encounter with the adulteress, encounter with the sinful woman in the pharisee's house, and healing of the paralytic) with three scenes that consummate mercy (anointing at Bethany, entry into Jerusalem, and last supper). See Bino 2008: 208–218.

> Now then go up (*ascende*) with [Christ] into the upper room .... Stand at a distance (*a longe sta*) and, like a poor man, ... stretch out (*extende*) your hand ..., let your tears declare (*prode*) your hunger. But when he rises (*surgens*) from table, girds himself (*se praecinxerit*) with the towel and pours (*posuerit*) water into the basin, consider (*cogita*) what majesty it is that is washing and drying (*abluit et extergit*) the feet of men .... Look and wait (*specta et expecta*) and, last of all, give (*praebe*) him your own feet to wash. (*Inst.Incl.*: 1066–1076; *R.R.*: 86)

The ways in which the avatar plays a scene are four: contemplation, participation, co-participation, and identification. Each corresponds to different degree of affective and performative immersion in the scenes of the memorial play, but they operate independently of its narrative arc: they do not unfold in step with the story's linear development; rather, they arise inside individual scenes. At times a scene is performed wholly in a single mode; at others the avatar plays through several, sometimes by steadily deepening immersion in the vision, sometimes by alternating immersion/emersion movements.

Contemplation is the first mode. Here the woman projects her first-person presence *into* the scene, yet her avatar remains inactive. The events are not narrated in detail; they are presented instead as strongly empathetic images, arranged paratactically. Scenes intended for *cogitare* – Christ's baptism, the forgiveness of the adulterous woman, the healing of the paralytic, Peter's betrayal, the *ecce homo* – are played in this way. Even so, the avatar's viewpoint is no mere bystander's: it stands in an affective relation to the people in the drama, seeing them close at hand, hearing them, watching them act, grasping their emotions, and sharing them. One example is the scene of Jesus before Pilate:

> Mark well how he stands before the governor: his head bent, his eyes cast down, his face serene, saying little, ready for insults and scourging. I know you can bear it no longer .... See now, after the scourging he is led forth wearing the crown of thorns and the purple robe. Pilate says: "Behold the man". (*R.R.*: 88–89)

The second mode is participation. The woman projects her first-person presence *into* the scene, and her avatar becomes a new character in the drama. The avatar inserts itself into the relationships already unfolding among the other figures, so that the episode departs from the Gospel narrative. Whenever a scene is played exclusively in this mode, the action always ends with the avatar 'at the Lord's feet'. Thus, when the Virgin visits Elizabeth, the avatar sees the two women embrace, joins them, then prostrates herself at their feet and venerates Jesus in Mary's womb. At the Nativity the avatar first acts as midwife, then lays the Infant in the manger and tenderly kisses his feet. In Gethsemane the avatar watches Christ pray in anguish and then enters the garden, licking the drops of blood that have fallen to the ground and wiping the dust from his feet with its lips. On Golgotha it witnesses the crucifixion from afar, then approaches the cross, stands with the Mother at the feet of the Crucified, and speaks to him. During the deposition, the avatar first observes Nicodemus remove the nails, then joins the action, licking the blood spilled on the ground and caressing the dust of Christ's feet. In every instance, the affective posture fashioned in the cell is now actively enacted.

Co-participation is the third mode in which the recluse projects her first-person presence into the scene. Yet, her avatar takes part by aligning its viewpoint with that of a character already on stage. What the avatar sees is subjective; what it feels is nonetheless first-person, for through an exercise in relational psychagogy it experiences the character's own sensations; and what it does are actions performed together *with* that character. Whenever a scene is played wholly in this co-participatory mode, the character accompanied is the Virgin. Thus, in the annunciation scene, the avatar enters Mary's room and reads the Scriptures with her, waits for the angel, sees him arrive and hears his greeting; it then imagines Mary's rapture as, "full of grace", she feels in heart and womb the presence of God while he takes flesh from her. In Jerusalem the avatar searches for the missing boy with the Mother, and, on finding him among the doctors in the Temple, weeps with her in relief. On Golgotha it approaches the cross with the Virgin, imagines her anguish, and together they shed tears of grief.

In three instances, however, co-participation deepens into identification, the fourth and final mode of playing a scene. The woman projects her first-person presence into the scene, her avatar accompanies the character and, by superimposing gaze upon gaze, it adopts that character's viewpoint, performs that character's actions, and feels that character's emotions. The first-person presence remains, but it is 'clothed' in another role and plays it in a personal way. Consequently, the recluse's postural figure is further shaped by the experience of identifying with the character. The three scenes the avatar plays in this way centre on three women: the penitent sinner who anoints Christ's feet in the Pharisee's house; Mary of Bethany who pours ointment on his head; and Magdalene who sees him risen. All follow the same pattern, yet the process of identification differs, altering the final affective posture the avatar assumes. Let us examine these scenes in detail.

First scene (*Inst. Incl.*: 987–1002). The avatar enters the Pharisee's house and conjures a vision of the Lord reclining at table (*recumbentem ibi Dominum tuum attende*). Its gaze aligns with that of the sinner as she approaches Jesus and kneels at his feet (*accede cum illa beatissima peccatrice ad pedes eius*). Immediately, the two viewpoints merge: the avatar is prompted to act in the first person, washing Christ's feet with tears, drying them with hair, covering them with kisses, and anointing them with ointment (*lava lacrymis, terge capillis, demulce osculis, et fove unguentis*). The fusion must be so complete that the avatar senses the fragrance of the balm upon itself (*nonne iam sacri illius liquoris odore perfunderis?*). From this point on, the avatar plays the role in the first person and enters into a direct relationship with Christ, reliving (and varying) the Gospel episode (Luke 7: 36–38) as its own plea for forgiveness:

> If he still will not let you approach his feet, be insistent, beseech him, raise your eyes to him brimming with tears and extort from him with deep sighs and unutterable groanings what you seek . . . . It will seem to you sometimes that he averts his gaze, closes his ears, hides the feet you long to touch. None the less be insistent, welcome or unwelcome, and cry out: "How long will you turn your face away from me? How long shall I have to cry out without your listening to me? Give back to me, good Jesus, the joy of your salvation". (*R. R.*: 83–84)

Second scene (*Inst. Incl.*: 1029–1060). The avatar enters the house of Lazarus, Martha, and Mary at Bethany, sees them at table with Jesus, and notes their roles: Martha serves, Lazarus is seated, and Mary takes a jar of ointment and pours it over Christ's head. The avatar is invited to join the banquet with joy (*gaude . . . huic interesse convivio*) and, explicitly, to assume Mary's role (*ungit Maria. Hoc . . . tuum est*). From that moment the action continues in the first person; however, because the avatar performs precisely Mary's actions, Mary herself becomes the recluse's avatar. She "breaks the jar of her heart" (*frange alabastrum cordis tui*) and pours its contents upon the Lord's head; she hears him rebuke Judas and the Pharisee who protest the waste of ointment; she sits silent at his feet and kisses them, lifts her eyes to gaze on him, strains her ears and listens to the one who has now become the bridegroom for whom the cell has prepared her.

Third scene (*Inst. Incl.*: 1207–1233). The avatar prepares the spices and goes to the tomb with Magdalene. Once there, the memory of what the woman saw with the eyes of the body renders the scene present, so that the avatar can now see it, in the first person:

> Now an angel sitting on the stone that has been rolled away from the entrance, now inside the tomb one angel where his head had lain, one where his feet, proclaiming the glory of his Resurrection, now Jesus himself looking with so gentle a gaze on Mary as she weeps for sorrow, and saying to her with so sweet a voice: "Mary". (*R.R.*: 91)

Then the avatar undertakes a psychagogic mnemonic exercise: it summons Magdalene's affective movements and feels them first-hand, bodily and in the first person:

> "Mary". At this utterance let all the floods burst forth, let tears stream up from the very bottom of your heart, let sighs and sobs issue from your inmost depths. ... What did you feel, when you prostrated yourself at this utterance and answered his greeting with the cry: "Master"? ... Tears preclude any further utterance as the voice is stifled by emotion and excess of love leaves the soul dumb, the body without feeling. (*R.R.*: 91)

Finally, when Christ forbids Mary to touch his feet, the avatar takes on Magdalene's role and responds in the first person, engaging him in a personal dialogue that, once again, enters the Gospel narrative (John 20: 17) and reshapes it:

> "Do not touch me", he says .... How is this, Lord? ... May I not touch, may I not kiss those lovable feet, for my sake pierced with nails and drenched in blood? ... But I will not let you go, I will not leave you, I will not spare my tears, my breast will burst with sobs and sighs unless I touch you. (*R.R.*: 92)

When Mary Magdalene – sent by Christ to announce his Resurrection to the disciples – returns to the tomb, Jesus now allows her to touch him. So, she comes forward and clasps his feet. In this final act, there is no longer any distinction between Magdalene, the recluse's postural figure, and the recluse herself: "Linger here as long as you can, virgin," Aelred urges, "let not these delights of yours be interrupted by sleep or disturbed by any tumult from without" (*R.R.*: 92). To see and to touch the risen Lord at close quarters is the culmination of the meditation on the past, but it is equally the goal of the cell's discipline – Lent preparing for Easter, the vigil preparing for the nuptials of the Resurrection.

In sum, the first meditation enacts the nuptial model of love – to which the rule aspires – within the re-presented past. It follows a clearly mnemonic itinerary designed to awaken an intimate affective relationship with Christ. The recluse undertakes that itinerary always in the first person: at one moment co-participating in the Virgin's *affectus*, at another stepping into the scene with the humble posture of a handmaid at Christ's feet. Yet, when she enters fully into memory, she assumes the role of three women (the converted sinner, Mary of Bethany, and Mary of Magdala) who, as Saxer (1959) showed, had already been merged by Gregory the Great into the composite figure of Mary Magdalene. Within the Cistercian affective aesthetics – what Nagy (2000: 276) calls a "flourishing of tears" – Magdalene became the emblem of the path of conversion, contemplation, and compassion by which humanity draws near to

God. Bernard and later Nicholas of Clairvaux linked her tears to the ointments poured on Christ's feet, head, and body – a circulation of fluids bound to the spiritual fecundity of the journey from sin to mystical union (Bino 2021b). Depicted as both penitent and bride in the office the Order dedicated to her (Scarcez 2014), Magdalene stood as an icon of repentance (weeping), humility (remaining at the feet), devotion (listening in silence), and familial intimacy (kissing and embracing). Aelred here reseparates the composite, redistributing the figure into three distinct women so as to map more precisely the movements of the *affectus* and to arrange them in a dramatic process of 'becoming Magdalene' that begins with vision, advances through desire, and culminates in delight.

In the end, the sensuous, affective image that concludes the meditation on the past bears the fragrance of ointments and the taste of kisses, tears, and blood – elements that render the two lovers mutually present and sensuously perceptible to one another (Olson 2017).

This felt presence makes Magdalene the anchoress's avatar persisting beyond the meditation itself.

3 Performing Emotions: Feeling Like the Mother

3.1 Dramatic Discipline

The second case on which I work shifts the production of the memorial play from a meditative, inner, and imaginative vision to a ritual, outward, dramatic action.

I examine here the *Ordo ad faciendum disciplinam* of the *Confraternita dei Disciplinati di Santo Stefano* in Assisi, a brotherhood closely linked to the Franciscan Order (1327–1329). This hitherto unpublished text – studied here for the first time – sets out in detail the emotional, verbal, and gestural 'script' by which the brethren carried out their collective penitential flagellation. Thanks to the unusually rich *corpus* of sources for this sodality – one of the oldest and best documented in Italy – we can reconstruct the timeframe and manner in which the rite was enacted on Good Friday, when the confraternity shut itself inside the oratory at Vespers to commemorate Christ's passion and death.[15]

---

[15] The *corpus* of sources comprises: 1327 statutes (hereafter *Statuti*) published by Frank (2011); the almost contemporary *Illuminati* codex (hereafter *Illuminati*; Terruggia 2017), which is a 'community book' that contains the lauds, two distinct types of Latin *lectiones* commemorating the Passion, and the *ordo* for the rite of *benedictio vestium*; later fragments from one or more *laudari* (Perugi and Scentoni 2007); and the confraternity inventories (Nerbano 2017). The *Ordo ad faciendum disciplinam* is preserved in Assisi, Archivio Capitolare di S. Rufino, MSS 20 and 21. An edition by Lucia Galbiati (with a historical-dramatic study by D'Acunto and Bino) is forthcoming. I cite it according to Galbiati's transcription of MS 20 (hereafter *Ordo*). All translations are my own.

Flagellation is not a practice in its own right, but rather the very heart of an office divided into three sections. The first comprises the recitation of prayers and psalms, and the donning of the confraternal habit: it involves the physical and spiritual operations by which the brethren bring *homo interior* and *homo exterior* into accord, preparing themselves for *commemoratio*. The central section is the enactment of memory in the strict sense (that is, the memorial play), articulated in two parts: first, meditative listening to the Passion narrative as declaimed aloud by one of the brethren; then, the singing of the *laude* paced by the strokes of the scourge. Finally, the third section consists of a sequence of prayers by which the brethren prepare to exit the rite and concludes with the removal of the confraternal habit.

Here, too, the same process recurs: the physical-sensory closure to the external world, the subject's psychosomatic preparation for the production of the memorial play, and the adoption of the postural figure with which the subject plays it. The re-presentational dynamic, however, operates according to the rite's 'aesthetic dispositive' (Ries 1993, Weyer-Menkhoff 2002, Bonaccorso 2013): as a performance capable not only of expressing but also of creating shared values and shaping social relations, the rite does not eliminate the subject's psychophysical sensitivity to material reality (the affective and bodily perception in relation to objects and other persons) but suspends its ordinary channels, re-activating it within an extraordinary, structured, and organised experience that gives perception a new form and effects its transformation.

Therefore, the analysis of the process must take into account four elements closely interwoven with one another.

First, the office is carried out by a group of laymen who constitute a 'relational community', grounded in the free and responsible sharing of the bond of brotherhood (*con-fraternitas*). The "confraternal choir" – to use Apollonio's term (1956: 71) – differs from the community-as-body of religious conceived as an organic unity, set apart from the world and shaped by a manner of life. It is a *we* composed of individuals who adopt a shared pattern of Christian behaviour that shapes their lives *within* the world. That pattern of behaviour forms the subject's identity within a continuous dialectical relation and exchange exterior–interior (life in the world-life in the choir) and individual-group.

Second, responding to the ritual dispositive, the exclusion of external reality takes the form of a regulated separation from the world's space and an ordered suspension of its temporal dimension, allowing the choir to enter the dimension of sacred space and the time of memory, producing an actual and active relation in presence with the divine.

Third, the efficacy of this production of presence extends beyond sacred space and ritual time: it continually re-forms the choir's shared pattern of behaviour and orients the actions the brethren undertake in social space and secular time.

Fourth, the memorial play is at once an exterior, collective experience and an interior, individual one. The whole choir 'plays the memory', following the same script of words, songs, emotions, gestures, and actions. Nevertheless, each brother produces his own mental vision of memory, into which he projects his psychosomatic presence; likewise, he performs the memory in the first person with his own body (he sings, prays, moves, and scourges himself), experiencing personal physical and emotional sensations. The theatre of the mind and the theatre of the body are interlinked in a performance that continually brings into play the dynamic of the outer-inner man and the individual-group dialectic, seeking their accord.

Thus, ritual practice sets in motion a re-presentational process that both presupposes and creates a dynamic of 'circular reciprocity' linking individual identity and belonging to the choir; historical and ritual time–space; individual and collective emotional posture; and the personal and the choral body, together with their respective perceptual experiences. This dynamic has affinities with Turner's idea of "communitas" (1969), developed in relation to the ritual process, and with the "autopoietic feedback loop" central to Fischer-Lichte's performance theory (2008): both are shared psychophysical experiences that entail a relational transformation (or continual re-negotiation) of personal identity. Yet the process I am analysing is distinctive, and the key to understanding it, I believe, lies in the Latin term *disciplina*.

Both in the text of the office and in other sources concerning the confraternity – especially the *Statuti*: 32 – *disciplina* denotes at once the confraternal manner of life (*vivendi modus et forma*) that the brethren have pledged to 'follow' (*sectari disciplinam*); the ritual devotion they are bound to celebrate (*facere devotam disciplinam*); and, finally, the practice of flagellation at the heart of the office (*apprehendere disciplinam*).

The polysemy of the term reflects a semantic layering built up over the centuries. The Middle Ages condensed two notions adopted from Greco-Hellenistic *paideia* into *disciplina*: first, 'teaching-and-learning' (with *discere* as teaching and *discipulus* as he who learns); and second, a *manner of life* (the individual's formation according to behavioural and moral norms aligned with a shared model of the common good). Stroumsa (2009) shows how, through by Jewish culture, ancient Christianity redefined *paideia* in relation to the new conception of the individual, founded on an idea of ontological likeness (the human person as a body–soul created by God in His image) which also entails an unbridgeable ontological distance (the image is like-and-not-equal to God). Said distance is further widened by sin (the human failure to recognise oneself as not-equal and therefore 'other' than God). The Incarnation placed the body at the centre of the definition of the person (the flesh is the axis of salvation) and made education a discipline of the self that entails *praxis* (doing) rather than *theoria* (seeing and thinking): it aims at the recovery of perfection through the complete transformation of the self in imitation of Christ, who is *disciplina Dei* in person. At the root of this discipline of the self lies the principle of conversion (*metanoia*) as awareness of dissimilarity from God resulting in repentance: "the turning toward God was foremost a return to oneself, an attempt to understand the nature of sins that has effaced (or at the very least obscured) the image of God that man was supposed to represent" (Stroumsa 2009: 16). Re-founded on the logic of conversion and ordered to the dramatic reorientation of the human being towards God – of which I have already spoken in the first part of this Element – *disciplina* acquired therapeutic values (the discipline of affections and actions as *medicina animae et corporis*) and came to be understood as a 'care' of the self within the wider context of mutual care among neighbours (charity or mercy).[16] In the monastic tradition, *disciplina* became the (virtually exclusive) instrument of common ascetic living, the perfect Christian life (Leclercq 1957, Knox 1994, Guijarro 2013). Through a centripetal process of semantic specification, the term came to designate, first, the rule (*disciplina nostri ordinis*); by extension, the specific economy of each rule (*disciplina corporalis et spiritualis*); and finally, the ensemble of ritual practices of penance and punitive correction. Among these, flagellation was regarded as perfect *disciplina*, because it imitates the Lord's redemptive suffering: to practise it was to undergo an experience of pain that educates the individual, redeems them from sin, orients them towards God, and brings them back to salvation, fostering the spiritual growth both of the person and of the community to which they belong (Leclercq 1962, Smith 2009).

---

[16] In Christian thought, the 'discipline of the self' always carries a communal value. In clarifying this, Stroumsa engages with the notions of discipline and care of the self by Foucault who "has proposed seeing in the Christian attitude toward the self ... a will to suppress the self ... or at least to integrate it within a much larger framework. ... Only in a sense Foucault was right. ... The accent placed on the human person as independent monad, alone responsible ... for care of itself is not found among Christians. But his insistence on the limitation, even the suppression of the self ... leads us along a false path. ... The Christian self does not disappear into the community; it becomes ... emblematic" (2009: 24–25). Asad's position is similar (1993: 112): "while Foucault seems to concentrate his attention entirely on a "microcosm of solitude," ... in the dominant form of medieval monasticism (cenobitic, as opposed to eremitic), the technology of the self ... is itself dependent on the institutional resources of organized community life". On the link between the therapeutic value of discipline and mercy in Augustine, see De Capitani 2018.

In our case the semantic process runs in the opposite direction: contemporaneous official documents – such as letters from bishops or papal legates – designate the brethren as *disciplinati* of the Crucified Christ precisely insofar as they are penitents who practise the devotion of the discipline in remembrance of the Passion.[17] In a centrifugal extension of meaning, *disciplina* denotes first and properly the penitential flagellation, then the office as a whole, and finally the confraternal manner of life. In all three cases it is a memory of the Passion.

The semantic reversal corresponds to an inversion of the re-presentational process. In the context of contemplative life (coenobitic or reclusive), the production of the memorial play is the culmination of a 'regular discipline' – what Asad (1993: 130) calls "the gradual reshaping of the self" – which orders the bodily operations and the interior exercises of virtue, directing them towards a precise relation with the divine that the devotee experiences in mnemonic meditation. By contrast, in the context of a lay, associational manner of life, the memorial play appears to be the starting point: it is the emotional, physical, active, sensual, and embodied experience of the Passion of Christ that enables the individual to bring his affective posture into accord with the gestures and actions he performs. By 'entering' the rite and playing the memory, he disciplines his psychosomatic unity through the collective, affective, and sensual experience of Christ's suffering, and gives form both to his identity as a member of the choir and to his way of being in the world.

In other words, the rite is a *dramatic discipline* of memory, virtually a "spiritual exercise" (in Hadot's sense, 1993) that embodies the choir's *devotio* to the Crucified Christ and translates it into an existential form.[18] The physical, collective performance has a psychagogic power: it produces the postural figure – the avatar – which, in this case, is an *emotional posture*, the attitude with which the choir plays the memory of the Passion, and which then becomes a daily *habitus*, individual and social.

Whichever avatar is configured, then, depends on the circumstances and contingencies of the ritual performance – that is, on the time of the rite (when the office is celebrated), its form (how it is celebrated), and, finally, the memory the rite renders present (the dramaturgical schema of the recollection of the Passion).

---

[17] See Sini 2011: 197–199, 203, 211–213, 242.
[18] Thomas Aquinas (*Summa Theologiae*, II–II, 94, a.1 ad 1) explains that *devotio* is the "*interior actus religionis*" by which a person devotes (*devovet*) the whole self to God – an interior disposition that issues in concrete practices of prayer and manner of life.

3.2 Dramaturgy of Time: The Choir's Good Friday

By shutting themselves within the oratory's 'sacred precinct' at Vespers on Good Friday, the choir creates the conditions to make the Passion of Christ present on the very day when memory brings it back into the present, thereby producing and enacting an actual presence of the event. However, the office of the discipline does not 'open' a ritual temporality but is 'set' within it: it is one scene in a dramaturgy of memory that the confraternity unfolds throughout the day.

The *Statuti* (60–62) set out the order of this dramaturgy, specify its places and devotions, and state its function: to conform both the individual and the choir to the Crucified Christ. Memory is articulated in temporal 'stations' corresponding to the canonical hours. At Matins the choir gathers in the oratory and, in secular dress, listens to "the Passion, the pains, and the sighs of Christ". At Prime, the brethren don the sodality's habit and go to the churches of San Francesco and Santa Maria degli Angeli (the Porziuncola), where they perform for the people (*populo representent*) "the lauds of weeping, the songs of sorrow, and the bitter laments of the Virgin Mother, widowed and deprived of her own Son". During the day they take part in the Liturgy of the Passion and hear the sermon with the civic community.[19] Finally, at Vespers the choir regathers in the oratory for the rite of discipline.

The result is a mnemonic itinerary in circular movement: entry into the confraternity's enclosed, private space (oratory), exit to the public civic celebration, then re-entry into the private sphere. This inside/outside/inside motion marks the exclusivity of the choir's devotions while situating them within the city: it underscores the confraternity's bond with the Franciscan community (the *laude* of weeping are sung at the Order's two chief sites) and its belonging to the ecclesial community (with which it joins for the Liturgy of the Passion and the sermon).

Moreover, the itinerary apparently entails different ways in which the individual and the choir participate in memory, marked by whether or not the confraternal habit is worn – a point to which I shall return next. The subject who listens to the Passion in the oratory without the habit is not a *disciplinato* but a devotee who belongs to a group; by contrast, the habit identifies him as a member of the choir when he re-presents Mary's weeping in public. When he takes part without the habit in the Church's rites and hears the sermon, he is a member of the Christian community; vesting in the habit to perform the

---

[19] By liturgy of the Passion I mean the ensemble comprising the euchological office, the Adoration of the Cross, and the Mass of the Presanctified, which the Roman-Seraphic Missal (in use at Assisi) prescribed at None (Van Dijk 1963: 241–244, Bino 2024b).

dramatic discipline makes him part of a collective, relational identity and assigns him a role within the ritual performance.

The modes of participation correspond to different degrees of activating the senses and emotions. Devout listening to the Passion appears as an interior, meditative exercise of affective preparation, both individual and choral. The public singing of the *laude* of the Mother's sorrow engages the whole body (voice, gesture, movement) but is above all an emotional performance aimed at arousing compassion in its audience – the *Statuti* (62) are explicit here, urging the brethren to perform the *laude* with greater attention to the emotional side than to words or voice (*magis ad lacrimas intendentes, quam ad verba vel voces*). Participation in the Liturgy of the Passion follows the dynamics of the psycho-physical engagement of the penitent, adoring assembly (La Salle 1997), as does the communal hearing of the sermon, often designed to elicit mass emotional responses centred on penance and compassion – "the grammar of Good Friday" preaching (Johnson 2012). Finally, the performance of the dramatic discipline is a synaesthetic experience that activates the inner senses and the whole body.

The structuring of memory by the canonical hours makes them the 'immediate' conduit between past and present, turning the itinerary into an episodic re-presentation of the events of the Passion, at the intersection of the monastic tradition of prayer and the Franciscan dramaturgy of meditation (Falvay 2025, and bibliography therein). Elsewhere I have shown – especially thanks to Bonaventure of Bagnoregio – that the Order's writers divided the Passion narrative into: arrest, mockery, and imprisonment (Matins); encounter with the Mother, trial, scourging-crowning with thorns and condemnation to death (Prime); ascent to Calvary, crucifixion and death (Terce and None); deposition (Vespers); burial (Compline) (Bino 2024a).

The office of the discipline is the concluding station of this itinerary into the memory of the Passion of Christ, first meditated in private, then re-presented and lamented in public, and finally celebrated and heard with the community. It is the choir's intimate liturgy with which the choir commemorate the hour of Vespers, making present the moment when Christ's dead body was taken down from the cross and placed in his Mother's arms as she, together with those who loved him, wept.

Thus, it is within the timeframe of these tears that the form of the rite and the mnemonic experience it produces are to be read.

3.3 Donning Compunction: Entering the Rite

As already noted, the office of the discipline is articulated in three moments: an entry, an exit, and – at the centre – the practice of penitential flagellation. The latter has its own complete structure, almost a 'rite within the rite' – copied independently both at the end of the two manuscripts that transmit the full *Ordo* and in the confraternity's 'community book' alongside readings and *laude* (*Illuminati*: 25 v–26 v).[20]

In the briefest terms, the overall schema of the Good Friday office is as follows:

Introit	Bell rings
	- Opening formula (*Adiutorium nostrum, Pater noster*);
	- Penitential act (*Confiteor, Misereatur, indulgentiam absolutionem, orationes*);
	Bell rings
	- Vesting (Psalm 50, *Miserere*, in responsorial form, *minister*-choir);
	- Genuflection and prayers for the dead (Psalm 126, *De profundis, orationes, Requiem*).
Rite of Flagellation	Opening formula (*Adiutorium nostrum, Apprehendite disciplinam*);
	- Silent recitation of the *Pater noster*, accompanied by collective flagellation;
	- Silent listening to the sung *lectiones latinae de planctu beatae Virginis*, entrusted to the lector;
	- Silent recitation of the *Pater noster*, accompanied by collective flagellation;
	Bell rings
	- Singing of the *laude de passione Salvatoris nostri Iesus et mestissime Matris eius*, entrusted to the cantor; between stanzas the choir performs the collective discipline;
	- Silent recitation of the *Pater noster*, accompanied by collective flagellation;
	Bell rings
	- Latin prayers, entrusted to the *minister*;
	- Silent recitation of the *Pater noster*, accompanied by collective flagellation;
	Bell rings
	- Fourteen vernacular prayers, recited by the *porrector preces*;

---

[20] The rite has a festal form, celebrated on Sunday mornings and on holy days of obligation, and a Passion form, celebrated on Friday evenings and on Good Friday. The general structure of the rite remains unchanged; the prayers, antiphons, readings, and *laude*, however, vary with the occasion.

	- Silent recitation of five *Pater noster* and five *Ave Maria*, accompanied by collective flagellation; Bell rings - Four vernacular prayers, recited by the *porrector preces*; - Collective flagellation after each prayer; Bell rings - Latin prayers; - Silent recitation of the *Pater noster*, accompanied by collective flagellation.
Dismissal	Prayers to Mary at the altar (*Ave Regina coelorum, Ave Maria*); - Three bell rings: at each, a genuflection with the recitation of the *Ave Maria*; Bell rings - Removal of the habit (during the recitation of the hymn *In passione Domini*); - Final blessing.

Beyond the rite's form, the *Ordo* details how it is to be celebrated. It distinguishes the parts assigned to the officiant (*minister*), lesson-reader (*lectionarius*), *cantor*, and prayer-reader (*porrector preces*) from those for the choir; specifies the vocal delivery of antiphons, psalms, prayers, and songs (in silence, in a low voice, or aloud); and notes the brethren's 'regulated gestures' – postures (kneeling, standing), proxemics (at one's place, at the altar), and the cues marking each transition (the bell).

Above all, the *Ordo* (4 r) states that flagellation is always a *fustigatio* "*in memoriam Passionis*", to be carried out "*humiliter*" and sung "*lacrimanter et pie*".

The introit prepares the brethren towards this intention in three stages. First, all acknowledge unworthiness and sins by mutual confession – the *Confiteor* recited by the *minister* and then the choir – with the accompanying absolution: the *Misereatur* and *indulgentiam absolutionem*; this penitential act delivers their souls from evil and re-orients them to the good (Schembri 1969). Next, each brother dons the confraternal habit to the alternating minister–choir chant of Psalm 50 (*Miserere*), thus assuming the interior penitential posture with which he enters the rite as a member of the choir. Finally, the choir genuflects towards the altar and recites Psalm 126 (*De profundis*), prayers for the dead, and the *Requiem*, thus reconstituting the community of living and dead – bound by the imperishable bond of brotherhood – and physically adopting the penitential posture with which it takes part in the mnemonic re-presentation.

The three phases of the introit correspond to penance understood as *conversio* (a change of mind, heart, and life), entailing reorienting the desiring tension from exterior to interior, from the world to God.[21]

The semantic pivot of this affective re-ordering is the ritual donning of the habit, quite different from the clerical liturgical vesting studied by Palazzo (2014). For the Assisi *disciplinati*, the sackcloth habit's specific meaning comes from the rite that blesses and bestows it at entry into the sodality (*Illuminati*: 28 r–v). It has three prerogatives: it is the *habitus* that outwardly displays (*sic induti exterius*) their having inwardly stripped off sin so as to be clothed with Christ (*interius induant Domini nostri Jesu Christi*); it is a bulwark against adversity; above all, it is the instrument by which God makes them His servants (*famuli*) and fills them with the grace of compunction whenever they wear it. In short, the habit is the sign of a penitential state including both contrition and compunction – two stages of "sorrow according to God" (Nagy 2000: 19) born of awareness of one's sins. If contrition is remorse for sin – an interior (spiritual, invisible) pain accompanied by the will to confess (Casagrande 2015: 308–319) – compunction is 'sensible repentance', the perpetual pain at the memory of sin that also carries desire for the Lord (Williams and Steenbrugge 2021). This 'feeling-in-action' – as Nagy shows (2000: 421–430) – is a repeated prick that becomes *habitus* and issues in tears, God's gift.

Thus, the introit is the spiritual and emotional process whereby the choir suspends their ordinary perceptual capacities and activates them within the extra-ordinary experience of ritual commemoration. In this process, wearing the habit marks the passage from *contritio* to *compunctio*: the adoption of the posture that enables the brethren to scourge themselves *lacrimanter* in remembrance of the Passion. At Vespers on Good Friday – the time of Mary's weeping over her Son's dead body – vesting reaches its fullest meaning and becomes *a clothing in tears to lament*. With this affective intention, the kneeling choir of penitents begins to play the memory.

3.4 Dramaturgy of Memory: Feeling Like the Mother

The memory of the Passion is re-presented in two timeframes, played on two planes: the interior vision produced by listening to the *lectiones de planctu beatae Virginis*, and the physical action of *fustigatio*, punctuating the vernacular performance of the *laude de passione Salvatoris nostri Iesus et mestissima*

---

[21] For an overview of the meaning of *conversio* in relation to penance, see Casagrande 2025: 45–49, and Milanese 2024, who also reconstructs the term's etymology and meanings.

Matris eius with scourge-strokes. In both cases the dramaturgy of memory is a lament. The diegetic dispositive, however, differs: the text guiding the interior vision *recalls pain*; the *laude* punctuated by flagellation are *the song of pain*. These dispositives yield two modes of memorial presence. On the one hand, the subject is projected into the past recalled by the Mother and sees the pain she feels for her Son's Passion, then and there; on the other, the subject re-enacts the memory in the present and weeps with the Mother, here and now. Although interdependent, the vision prepares the re-enactment. Let us see how.

The Latin readings, heard by the choir in silence, form a long verse narrative in which Mary recalls her Son's sufferings in nine tableaux, from the Sanhedrin trial to the burial.[22] Her gaze gives the memory locative, temporal, and dramatic shape, which she re-lives from within, as a character – both witness and actor. Thus, the Gospel Passion is modified and expanded, drawing on Scripture and on exegetical, meditative, and sequence traditions.[23] The scenes are constructed from the maternal viewpoint, largely in the first person, and follow a five-part sensory, emotional, and physical score. First, Mary's gaze establishes the setting – where she is, what she does, what occurs around her. Second, her sensory perception registers what befalls her Son, chiefly through hearing and sight. Third, perception yields an image: she narrates what the Son suffers and at whose hands. Fourth, the image elicits an inner emotion in her, which she verbalises, naming her pain. Fifth, that inner pain produces tears (varying in intensity and hue) and a bodily response – articulated in voice/speech, gesture, posture. I present the composition of the Sanhedrin scene, where both the locative-temporal dynamics of the gaze and the score linking sensory perception, emotional response, and bodily reaction are clearly legible:

> I stood before the doors of the temple, overwhelmed by desolation (*desolata vehementer*).... I heard (*audiebam*) the cries of the Jews, the scribes, and the

---

[22] Although unpublished, the text is preserved in the confraternity's 'community book' and photo-reproduced in *Illuminati*: 19r–25r. It is the earliest attestation of what Pellegrini (2013) – who studied the only known vernacular version – called the *Planctus Magistrae Doloris*, elsewhere termed the devotion of the 'ten sorrows of Mary *in morte filii*' or *Purpura Mariae*. Eleven witnesses are known (one coeval, from the Franciscans of the Sacro Convento, Assisi), all from the fourteenth and fifteenth centuries (see Bino 2019 and bibliography). The text hybridises the sequential *planctus* – a brief melic composition on the Mother's tears beneath the cross, at the deposition, and at the tomb (Sticca 1984, Bino 2008, Kubartová Poláčková 2023) – with a euchological-meditative form that sets the Passion in episodes. It appears to be a lyrical reworking of the *Liber de passione Christi et doloribus et planctibus Matris eius* (the *Quis dabit*), late twelfth century, part of the *Tractatus in laudibus sanctae Dei genitricis* attributed to the Cistercian Oglerio of Lucedio (Marx 2025).

[23] Seminal studies by Pickering (1970) and Marrow (1979) established that expansion of the Passion narrative began in the patristic period through typological scriptural citation. The late Middle Ages innovated by drawing on Old Testament materials – especially Isaiah, the Psalms, and the prophets – to forge a highly emotive narrative.

Pharisees who ... mocked (*illudebant*) my Son ..., covering his face with spittle. At a column of the temple they bound my Son, and with rods they struck his most holy body; the impious smote his cheeks with wicked hands.... So I stood outside, weeping (*plorans*) and lamenting (*eiulans*) in bitterness of heart (*in amaritudine cordis*): I bathed my cheeks with tears, struck my breast with my hands, and all my limbs seemed to weep (*flere videbant*).... Then the door of the temple opened: behold, they bring my Son, surrounded by a multitude of armed men, his hands bound like a robber's. And when I saw him (*vidissem*) bound in so shameful a way, all my inward parts were stirred (*commota sunt omnia viscera mea*) and my heart failed (*elanguit cor meum*) for the greatness of the pain (*pre multitudine doloris*).... I saw him (*videbam*) already as dead, and through excessive anguish (*pre nimia angustiam*) ... my throat had become mute (*mute facte erant fauces mee*). (*Illuminati*: 19 r–20 v)

This score articulates the Passion's dramaturgy on two mirroring narrative levels: the emotional script of the Virgin's grief, and the account of Christ's bodily pain. The first mediates the second – visually (it produces an image of Jesus's wounded body) and expressively (it translates pain into gesture and bodily reaction) – rendering sensible and perceptible what is otherwise inaccessible: physical pain, as Scarry (1985) notes, is perceivable only to the sufferer. Yet this is neither a mere mediation of Christ's suffering humanity nor a generic maternal sorrow. The bond between Mary and Christ is unique: as his sole earthly parent she is the "source of his humanity", and he is "bone of her bones and flesh of her flesh" (Fulton Brown 2002: 452–453). Theologically grounded between the eleventh and twelfth centuries, this bond becomes central in Franciscanism (Santi 2020, De Dominicis 2024), making Mary's suffering the medium of a *pain shared and co-felt* in the same flesh, and impressing on the listener a model of *perfect empathetic love*.

The devotee enters the drama of memory through the Mother's eyes, yet he does not adopt her gaze: he does not play it in co-participation (subjective viewpoint) or in identification (first-person shot). Instead, Mary's emotional script elicits in him a *pain response* parallel to that expressed by her in words and bodily gestures. In other words, the devotee does not assume the Mother's avatar 'within the scene'; he is guided to respond, by degrees, to the Passion-pain she feels.

By degrees. Mary's pain is of two kinds and elicits in the devotee two distinct emotional responses. On the one hand, compassion: co-participation in the visceral physical pain by which the Mother shares the Son's torment. On the other, lamentation: sharing Mary's mourning as she weeps over the Son's broken flesh, taken down from the cross and prepared for burial – a universal mourning that no longer follows the ancient logic of exclusive kinship, of blood lineage (*ghenos*), as described by Loraux (1990), but an inclusive kinship grounded in all's participation in Christ's blood and flesh.

These responses are mediated by two distinct re-presentational processes that divide the Passion narrative in two sections.

From the crowning with thorns to the crucifixion, Mary co-suffers Christ's pains and describes pain entering her through the senses, generating *amaritudo* and *angustia*, both modalities of his Passion. *Amaritudo* recalls the taste of the gall he drank on the cross – the taste of human sin he cleanses with his blood (Ziolkowski 2003); it afflicts the Mother's heart and draws tears that overflow to blindness. *Angustia* is the feeling of mortal peril with no escape (Haubrichs 2003). It works on Mary's body, twisting her entrails, wounding her heart, corroding her limbs, draining their strength to nothing. This twofold emotional effect is clear in the scene where Christ is mocked, crowned with thorns, robed in purple, and scourged before her eyes:

> Before me (*coram me*) they crown him with thorns, strike him with the reed, strip him of his garments, and clothe him in purple. . . . I saw all this with my own eyes (*cum ista viderem oculis meis*), and I wept for the most bitter pain (*amaritudine flebam*). My soul was in anguish (*angustiabatur anima mea*); my heart was pierced by the lance of pain (*iaculo doloris findebatur*). (*Illuminati*: 20 v–21 r)

The psychosomatic dynamic of compassion is perfectly rendered in the scene of Christ's condemnation to death, which first sets out the progression hearing → emotion → bodily reaction:

> After I heard that my Son had been judged guilty of death and was to be hung upon the wood of the cross, my soul was greatly troubled for the excess of pain (*conturbata est anima mea pro nimio dolore*); within me my heart was overturned (*subversum cor meum in memet ipsa*), the senses of my heart were disturbed (*sensus cordis mei conturbati sunt*); I fell to the ground – collapsed to the earth – for the greatness of my anguish (*propter magnitudinem angustiae*); my eyes did not cease from tears, my face was swollen from weeping (*facies mea intumuerat a fletu*), and the light of my eyes was darkened by the great abundance of tears (*lumen oculorum meorum obscuratum erat propter multitudinem lacrimorum*). (*Illuminati*: 21 v–22 r)

Then it describes the sequence seeing → emotion → bodily reaction that brings about the annihilation of the Mother's body:

> They brought my Son before me (*ante me*), between two robbers, his hands bound, crowned with thorns. And as I saw all this with my own eyes, my whole soul was melting (*tota liquefiebat anima mea*); within I was wholly aflame (*tota intus urebar*) from the intensity of the anguish (*pre angustie magnitudine*). Almost dead (*quasi mortua*) and as if consumed (*pene*

consumpta), I was carried by others: for the immensity of the pain had destroyed the body's strength (*viris corporis exterminaverat magnitudo doloris*), and the anguish of the mind had exhausted the body's limbs (*membra corporis debilitaverat angustia mentis*). (*Illuminati*: 22 r)

The sharing of the Passion reaches its apex at the crucifixion, where the sight of the Son upon the cross and the blood flowing from his wounds engenders in Mary an interior suffering that takes on the tones of the torment of the flesh, to the point that she feels her heart crucified with him and physically pierced by the sword:

> My soul suffered in torments (*torquebatur*); I contemplated (*considerabam*) my Son and saw (*videbam*) the fount of blood flowing from his limbs; and my heart was crucified (*cruciabatur cor meum*), and I felt the cruel sword of sorrow (*crudelem gladius doloris*) – which the holy old man Simeon had foretold – passing through my soul (*transire per animam meam sentiebam*). (*Illuminati*: 23 r)

From this point the re-presentational process shifts and – almost in a cross-fade – lamentation overlays compassion. Mary no longer mediates the Son's pain by describing her own; rather, through tears she gives voice to his agonising body, addressing first the tormentors (exhorting them to penance), then the women who accompany her (inviting them to weep). When death ends Christ's sufferings, compassion recedes, and lamentation takes its place. The narration shifts to the third person and proceeds on two planes: on the one hand, the relation between Christ's lifeless flesh and Mary's; on the other, the emotional reactions of those who see – or are called to see – their bond of love and share it in weeping. Three scenes follow. The first shows Mary, crucified in soul, lying dead before the cross from which her lifeless Son hangs:

> The Virgin Mary stood dead before the cross (*mortua ante crucem stetit*), so that she could not speak, nor did she seem to breathe. . . . Consider how great the pain of seeing Jesus hanging on the cross (*pendentem in cruce*) . . . and the Mother . . . lying before the cross (*iacentem ante crucem*), crucified in soul by the sword (*spirituali gladio crucifixam*). (*Illuminati*: 24 r)

The second depicts the intimacy between Mary's flesh and Christ's: first the Mother throws herself upon her Son's corpse, taken down from the cross, covering his wounds with kisses and embraces; then she wrests his body from those wrapping it for burial, unbinding his limbs from the bands:

> When he had been taken down, she flung herself (*irruit*) upon her Son's body, weeping most bitterly. Now she kissed the wounds of his head, now that of his side, then kissed and embraced the wounds of his hands and feet . . . . While they were wrapping some of his limbs and sought to bind the rest, she loosed

> the bands . . . . And all beside her stood in great, bitter sorrow. With difficulty they tore Jesus' body from his Mother's hands. (*Illuminati*: 24 v)

The final scene depicts the Mother's parting from her Son's body at the tomb. In an interplay of looks and weeping, Mary's grief spreads to all and turns her very flesh into eyes, dissolved in tears.

> Having come to the place of the sepulchre, they wished to bury him, but the Mother wept and would not allow it. . . . And seeing the Mother's sorrow, they wept with her: oh, what it was to see the Virgin Mary weeping! All her flesh seemed to have become eyes (*tota caro ipsius videbatur oculi facta*); she seemed all about to dissolve into tears (*videbatur tota lacrimis dissolvenda*). (*Illuminati*: 25 r)

The image of the Virgin becoming a weeping eye brings the listening to the *lectiones* to a close.

If the rite's introit reorients the choir's perceptual capacities and clothes it in tears of compunction, the first act of the memorial play is an affective path that shapes those tears first as compassion, then as lamentation. The latter becomes the posture with which the choir plays the second act of the memorial play. At the sound of the bell, flagellation begins.

3.5 Discipline of Compassion: Mercy

The *Ordo* (4r) states that the *laude*, paced by *fustigatio*, are meant to move the brethren's hearts to weeping (*movere corda fratrum ad planctum*). Flagellation is thus an explicitly emotional and transformative practice: a physical act that stirs inner emotion and alters the psychosomatic state.

However, this is not distinctive. Such psychagogic–transformative power characterises medieval flagellation, whether imposed as corrective punishment or self-inflicted as expiatory, conformative penance. Historical–anthropological studies concur that it functions as a discipline of personal identity, seen either as a ritual of communal shaping (Smith 2009); or as an educational instrument where the body serves as a semiophoric medium, that is, the flesh carries meaning (Vandermeersch 2002, Mills 2005); or a Maussian "technique of the body" (Mauss 1935). Notably, Largier (2007) stresses the tight soul-body relation and its shifting dynamics with changing practices and cultural contexts; Merback (2007) and Nagy (2022) focus on sense-emotion in lay mass flagellations and their effects on spectators.

The distinctive feature of the Assisi *disciplinati*'s flagellation lies elsewhere – namely, in the *dramaturgy* that shapes the mnemonic process and steers its psychagogic–transformative dynamic. Scholarship shows that, between the twelfth and fourteenth centuries and from central–northern

Italy, penitential flagellation became a Christo-mimetic mnemonic practice oriented to compassion.[24] Imitating Christ's scourging – the metonym of his suffering – the devotee enacts voluntary mortification of the flesh, reparative penance for sin, and a sharing in the Lord's wounds, thereby gaining access to redemption. Despite differences of setting, both monastic ritual flagellation (paradigm: Peter Damian) and lay devotional flagellation (private and public) are governed by a *dramaturgy of suffering flesh* that collapses distance from the devotee: he re-lives the Lord's pains in the first person, feeling them in his own body, in an *identificatory mode* Panofsky (1927) called "contemplative immersion". Here discipline is understood as a psychosomatic experience of retributive conformity ordered to salvation.

In Assisi, the confraternal flagellation is a mnemonic practice shaped by a *dramaturgy of tears*. Its intention remains compassion, yet it urges the devotee to relive Christ's pains by adopting Mary's emotional posture, according to an *empathetic mode* that takes the Mother's pain as the experiential model. It is therefore necessary to understand the diegetic economy of the *laude* – what they represent and *how* – as the ritual flagellation's intention and its psychosomatic discipline depend on it.

We do not know which of the five *de passione* pieces in the community book accompanied the flagellation.[25] However, they all share the same dramaturgic scheme: laments in which the Virgin, through tears, composes the image of Christ's body 'becoming' wounded and dolorous. All also explicitly solicit sharing her weeping: sometimes the choir asks Mary to *show* the Son's pain so they may weep with her; sometimes Mary asks the brethren to weep with her so that they may *see* his pains. Showing in order to lament, lamenting in order to see: the lament is no longer the response to the Mother's pain (as in the *lectiones*) but the *dispositive of empathetic perception* that mediates the vision of the Passion. The *laude* do not present Mary's suffering as such, but the image of the *vir dolorum* that she assembles and offers to the devout so that – looking through her sorrowing gaze – they may see and feel in the first person what he endured.

If we shift from purely textual dynamics to the ritual script in which the *laude* are performed, the lament becomes the intention with which the devotee performs the *fustigatio*: the empathetic dispositive is re-located into the action and shapes it. He scourges himself weeping with the Mother and, while feeling the pain of the lashes, aligns her point of view 'in subjective shot', he follows the line of her gaze, seeing in first person Christ bound, struck, scourged,

---

[24] The bibliography is extensive; for an up-to-date synthesis, see Chen (2018).
[25] It is the *laude* 1, 2, 3, 10, and 14 of *Illuminati*.

crowned with thorns, mocked, humiliated, crucified – the whole deformation of the God-man's body into the 'man of sorrows'. In scourging himself, he does not perform an analogical–fictional mimetic action (he does not imitate the mother's gestures) nor identifies with Christ; rather, he makes the body "an avenue to knowledge. Knowledge of the body, of the soul, of the truth, of reality, and of God" (Cohen 1995: 52–53). Perceiving Christ's pain through Mary's gaze – the medium of perfect empathy that fuses two into one and allows to say "I am you" (Fulton Brown 2002: 461–470) – the devotee gains access to the affective God-human bond: likeness. At the same time, he recognises that Christ's deformed body is the mirror – both consequence and reparation – of his own deformity as sinner, thereby grasping the nature of sins unlikeness from God. In sum, by becoming the dispositive for empathic perception of the Passion, maternal weeping reconfigures and transforms flagellation from a Christo-mimetic expiatory sharing into a dramatic discipline of knowledge and psychosomatic conformation.

Three aspects characterise it.

The first concerns the meaning and function of the *vir dolorum* image, fashioned by the *laude* and the end towards which the mnemonic process tends. That image must be read within Franciscan spirituality and within the Order's catechetical–pastoral programme – the matrix of the values inspiring the confraternity and its devotions. Recent studies show that early Franciscanism (late thirteenth to early fourteenth centuries) did not construe it in doloristic terms, nor as an image of redemptive violence (Bartolomei Romagnoli *et al.* 2024). Rather, it was understood as the image of God's radical, complete self-revelation and of his love *per Verbum crucifixum*.[26] Through the Passion and on the Cross God brings His *kenosis* to fulfilment and hands Himself over to humankind, fully sharing the flesh. From the word of the Cross that spoke to Francis, the human being begins to grasp the mystery of salvation and return *ad Verbum*. To set the *vir dolorum* before one's inner and outer gaze does not prompt mortification of the flesh, but the full restoration of the image of God in the person – soul and body.[27] If, as Coccia (2009: 158) notes, the Passion is the meeting-place of God and the human – so, "to suffer

---

[26] Here I refer to Bonaventure's theology of the Word: God 'goes forth from himself' and communicates through the *Verbum* – in creation (*per Verbum increatum*), in participation with the creature (*per Verbum incarnatum*), and finally in the Cross's radical self-revelation (*per Verbum crucifixum*) (Maranesi 2005).

[27] Here we also take up Bonaventure's re-interpretation of Augustine's *imago Dei*, a hallmark of much Franciscan anthropology (Delio 1999): the human being is created, body and soul, in the *imago Dei* – the Son. Thus, the human falls into sin and is deformed, body and soul; and regains likeness, body and soul, by imitating the Incarnate Word, most fully revealed on the Cross.

means, for God, to become human; for the human, to imitate God" – then, discipline *in memoriam Passionis* is a process of *conformatio*, compassion a *via transformationis*, and Mary's sorrow the gnoseological and affective dispositive mediating that encounter.

The second aspect is the esoteric character of this dramatic discipline and its refusal of a mimetic–spectacular dispositive. Unlike Umbrian flagellant processions and other contemporary confraternal practices, the brethren of Santo Stefano do not assimilate their bodies "to the pathetic vision of the suffering Christ", becoming "living images of piety" in a public spectacle of pain (Merback 2007: 143). For them, flagellation is a memory played within the choir and behind the oratory's closed doors: it may elicit a mutual "intervisual experience" of pain, not to be intended as a "real-time staging of Passion imagery" (166), but a real-time experience of compassion. The Virgin's weeping is the performative dispositive of Assisi's *disciplinati*. It is so, too, on Good Friday morning, when they don the habit of compunction and re-present Mary's laments to the people by singing *laude* of her sorrow without scourging. Nerbano (2015: 263) sees this Marian-lament centrality as the hallmark of Assisi's 'theatre of devotion', and traces it to the influence of Franciscan spirituality, where praise is the chief instrument of devotion and preaching. By making Mary's weeping the emotional script of Christ's pains, the Assisi brethren turn Good Friday memory into a shared *weeping of the Passion*, in private and in public.

Lastly, the third aspect is the outcome of this dramatic discipline: mercy. The Assisi rite stands within the Umbrian–Marchigian tradition of self-inflicted penitential flagellation, yet renews it. It preserves both Peter Damian's understanding of *verberatio* as configurative imitation, and the pacifying aim of the 1260 flagellant processions. The *Statuti* (33–36) make conformity to the Crucified Christ and the building of peace, respectively, the personal end of each brother and the choir's principal charge. Yet both aims are reinvented through Mary's 'perfect compassion', which has no penitential or retributive stamp (Mary is 'perfect humanity', without sin), but sharing and co-participatory ones. The nature of maternal compassion is most clearly understood through the Christian notion of *misericordia* (mercy). Beyond Greek – and modern – notions of pity (*eleos*, emotional sharing among kin/allies) or lament (*oiktirmos*, the sharing of tears), Christian *misericordia* is pain that is both empathic and generative. It recalls *splangchnizomai*, namely the pangs of childbirth: in the Synoptic Gospels it is used solely to describe Christ's compassionate response to human suffering (Köster 1979: 919). The pain Mary mediates to the devout is Christ's 'divine' and generative pain – the *angustia passionis* that brings forth the new self and Anthony of

Padua compares it to the *angustia parturientis*.[28] Therefore, *misericordia* denotes the spasm of the womb and the breaking heart of one who lives another's pain in his own flesh and aids the neighbour (as Augustine states plainly, *Sermo 358/A*). To adopt Mary's empathic gaze and make it the experiential dispositive of flagellation is to turn it into an embodied experience that disciplines both individual and choir to mercy, felt in interpersonal relations and practiced in communal and civic *works*.

Thus, mercy is the key term for grasping the ultimate sense of the Assisi brethren's dramatic discipline as a spiritual exercise that shapes the choir for the mutual care of neighbours.

The *Ordo* lays out this disciplining process: on entering the rite, the penitents ask God for mercy (*Misereatur nobis*) and invoke it by vesting in compunction (*Miserere*); they then interiorise it as an empathic response to the Mother's shared pain; finally, they experience it by seeing and feeling 'like the Mother' the life-giving pain of the Passion. By virtue of this psychosomatic co-feeling, in the final part of the rite they petition for peace, charity, justice, wisdom, and, at last, grace and salvation. They then leave the rite with a gesture that mirrors, and reverses, their entry: while reciting a hymn to the Passion – bitter and sweet, sorrowful and glorious – they remove the habit of compunction.

Disciplined to mercy, the brethren put their *habitus* into play in Francis's city. There, from the late thirteenth to the early fourteenth centuries, the pastoral and politico-institutional action of the Franciscan bishop Teobaldo Pontano (1296–1329) appears to reshape the city according to a penitential and associative model aimed at peace and mercy (D'Acunto 2010).[29]

The empathetic performance of flagellation as a discipline of compassion is best – and perhaps *only* – understood within that Assisi context, and it can also cast new light on the meaning of the confraternal *modus vivendi*, which is not a flight from the world but the lay, social construction of community. Of this care for the common good, Mary, Mother of Mercy, is the avatar: emotional posture and *forma formans*.

---

[28] The idea of *angustia passionis* as *angustia parturientis* recurs frequently in Anthony of Padua's sermons. See, for example, the General Prologue to his *Sermones dominicales et mariani* (Costa et al. 1979: 2): "Our soul is called the fruit of birth – that is, of the Lord's pain – for he fashioned it in the distress of the Passion, like a woman in labour."

[29] The clearest signs of this friar-bishop's programme are the 1310 institutionalisation of the so-called Pardon of Assisi – a plenary indulgence for all who, repentant and confessed, visited the Porziuncola; commissioning Giotto's *Magdalene* cycle (model penitent-lover) in a chapel of the Lower Basilica, while Lorenzetti frescoed the *Passion* on the left transept in the last years of his episcopate (1326–1328); and lastly, consolidating a network of confraternities he 'founded', giving them statutes and a seat (Brufani 1989: 47–48).

4 Epilogue

By analysing the anchoress's meditation and the Assisi confraternity's flagellation rite, I examined two distinct dynamics by which the faithful make themselves present within an imaginative encounter with Christ and live it sensually and emotionally.

The two experiences stand opposed in subject (a woman enclosed from the world vs a group of laymen living within it); in process (the memorial play as the telos of an individual's psychosomatic discipline or as a dramatic discipline of psychosomatic identity in its own right); in re-presentational dynamic (the avatar as a postural figure projected into the imaginal environment or as an empathetic posture adopted to enact a performance); and in relational outcome (a spousal affective relation vs a maternal empathetic one).

Both presuppose a dialectic between exterior and interior senses and emotions, evident in the structured process by which the subject's psychophysical sensorium is closed or suspended to everyday material reality and opened or activated to an extra-ordinary spiritual reality. In other words, they require a reconfiguration of perception that reverses sensory-affective direction from exterior to interior, in the service of disciplining the gaze and the person (recomposed in the indivisible unity of body and soul).

Section 1 set out the conceptual tools of the analysis and argued that this reversal – *ex parte spectantis ad partem agentis* (from spectator to performer) – corresponds to a dramatic dispositive of knowledge, theorised since the patristic era and anchored in Christian epistemology. From that way of seeing 'from-within, at-close-range' – typical of Western medieval Christianity at least until the Reformation – follow the two guiding ideas of this Element: *vision as action*, which makes the gaze a performative instrument; and *re-presentation as a process of production of presence*.

In the Prologue I argued that performance is a transdisciplinary hermeneutic framework for medievalists: it lets us read the agentive, experiential, and synaesthetic dimensions of texts, images, devotions, and rites, and it highlights the otherness of medieval forms of dramatic representation – the so-called 'sacred theatre' and 'liturgical drama' – whose canonical (and ambiguous) labels presuppose a modern notion of analogical–fictional reproduction.

As I write this Epilogue, Lauren Mancia publishes her Element, *Embodied Epistemology as Rigorous Historical Method*, in which she argues – carefully and persuasively – for a rigorous performative approach to the study of pre-modern devotional experience, especially monastic. She calls for an embodied, from-within approach, not merely an intellectual, external, and detached one. An exclusively rational – and academically impassive – historical method, she contends, cannot recover the lived interiority of religion as "genuine emotional and spiritual experiences". Shifting to the side of the action, by contrast, is an effective way "to disarm audiences' modern conceptions of the past" (Mancia 2025: 3–4): it enables us to trace devotional experiences and visions that were themselves embodied and performed, truly engaging bodies, senses, and emotions. Mancia therefore recommends the "reperformance" (note: not re-enactment or impersonation) "of historical actions ... as a scholarly method" (14–15).

Strikingly, this methodological destination was my point of departure. Since my doctorate in theatre history and for over twenty-five years, I have worked on the re-performance of (Western and Eastern) medieval Christian meditative, *laude*, and homiletic texts in churches and oratories, as well as in squares and workplaces. Precisely the empirical recognition of how these texts operate – activating a participatory mechanism of affective relationality so unlike the Renaissance theatre I studied – led me to seek its causes: first by adopting a dramaturgical mode of textual analysis (treating the texts as 'scripts'), then by studying the theoretical construction of the dramatic dispositive.

The synthesis, however, is the same: medieval religious experience entails an interior, agentive gaze, giving the experience its form and efficacy.

4.1 Embodying Vision

One might object that the performative gaze's efficacy is somewhat compromised by excluding material reality. If that exclusion is the condition for producing what I have called the *medieval avatar*, perhaps what results is not a fully real presence but only a mere 'feeling of being there' and acting.

The crux, however, lies in the dramatic strategy of re-presentation, tied to two paradigms of Christian "participatory mediality" identified by Christian Kiening (2019): the universal mediation whereby creation makes God present to the world as Creator; and the absolute mediation whereby Christ makes God present to humankind through the *communicatio* of the divine and human substance in his person (the unconfused unity). In both cases the mediation is paradoxical: it entails the presence, visibility, and tangibility of what is absent, invisible, and intangible.

Above all, it entails the human capacity to apprehend the presence of absence and, in turn, to render oneself present within mediation by reconfiguring one's psychosomatic faculties. I use *reconfiguration* in the etymological sense of *figura* derived not from Greek *typos* but from *schema*: it denotes the 'manner' in which something manifests its form in accord with 'what it is' and thus presupposes a gnoseological dispositive able to participate in the manifestation of being. Consequently, one who changes the *figura-schema* is *trans-formed*; one who loses it is *de-formed* (*aschematos* corresponds to Latin *turpis*) (Bino 2020).

Within this process, the exterior-interior, closure-openness dynamic with which I began becomes decisive. I clarify this with reference to modern media to which the notion of the avatar – at least in part – points (see Section 1, §4).

That dynamic follows Francesco Casetti's *projection/protection complex*: a mechanism "of disconnection and reconnection with reality that emerges thanks to enclosures and screens" (Casetti 2023: 34). It aims "at creating a 'protected' confrontation with the world and at the same time at 'projecting' individuals beyond the safe space in which they are located" (Casetti 2023: 14). Christian imaginative experience realises this complex insofar as it presupposes an intentional severance from the world which enables the subject to re-appropriate the world itself through a different configuration of vision. On the one hand, closure 'protects' the individual from simulacral exposure to the world (the illusion of appearances); on the other, re-presentation repairs the oppositional fracture between seeming and being (*duplicitas*), enabling the grasp of their unity (*simplicitas*).[30] In short, excluding external reality conditions a participatory mediation that projects the individual *into* a synaesthetic experience of the transcendent made present and trains the gaze to look *beyond the screen* of the merely visible.

The medieval avatar is the outcome not of a simulacral process but of reconfiguration, whereby the subject enters – and is immersed in – a participatory relation to the experience of God. In the two cases examined, the avatar engages the subject's physical body in two distinct ways. In the first, the affective projection of presence intro-flexes the body (bends it inward) and moulds it (disciplines it); in the second, the body itself produces a somatic presence of the *affectus*, disciplining itself through action. The body's affective introflexion and the emotions' bodily extroflexion are complementary processes in a production of presence of oneself – to oneself, and to God – that is at once a form of knowing and a manner of life.

This complementarity is especially clear in (direct and indirect) accounts of mystical dramatic vision, where vision is embodied as transformative action.

---

[30] In a passage of *De vera religione* (49:95), Augustine states plainly that the danger of simulacral exposure is perceptual illusion and the consequent loss of contact with reality. The individual exposed to perceptual *phantasmata* (namely to *what merely appears*) risks substituting them for reality to the point of no longer seeing it. The *phantasmata* become perceptual obstacles that "confront one on the way and do not allow one to pass" (*in itinere occurrunt et transire non sinunt*). To see, he concludes, one must "beware of simulacra" (*cavete a simulacris*).

An exemplary case is the hagiographic account of Catherine of Siena. If we read Raymond of Capua's *Legenda maior* (1395) as a dramatic, psychosomatic script, it is governed by two patterns: that of mind/spirit and that of the body. On the one hand, Catherine's interior experience intensifies as she is ever more absorbed in inner images and emotions; on the other, her body undergoes a gradual *diminutio* as she loses awareness of the exterior world. This cross-fade between perceptual introversion and the embodiment of inner vision is cast in two acts.

In the first act, Catherine leaves the familial and social logic that would form her as a virgin for marriage and withdraws into the 'inner cell' she herself builds as the intimate space for union with Christ, the bridegroom *par excellence*. Her withdrawal is more than removing the body from the world's order to be reborn into a spiritual order: it is *denegatio* of self – abandoning a self-consciousness conceived 'from and for itself' to assume a consciousness 'of the self in relation to God'. Fittingly, the itinerary towards union begins with a vision of Christ in Majesty whose effect is *self-forgetting*; proceeds through rites of passage (the vow of virginity, prayer and penitential action, reception of the penitents' veil); culminates in a sapiential revelation (in which Christ himself discloses the principles of self-knowledge and union); and ends with Catherine's mystical nuptials with Christ.

The second act concerns the experience of spousal life: she cleaves to the bridegroom with her whole self – mind, body, affections, and deeds. The visionary experience felt in the flesh overlaps with a desensitised bodily state, brought on by total fasting, sleeplessness, and dulled physical perception. This is not a negation of the body but its transformation through concrete care for the neighbour. Catherine learns to love as Christ and, in a conformative itinerary, ascends the Crucified as ladder and assimilates him as food: from him, she receives the crown of thorns, is clothed in his blood, feeds at his side, welcomes his heart into her breast, is pierced in the hand by the nail of the Passion; finally, she receives the stigmata. That final, public scene seals the unitive process. The embrace of the cross is almost a Eucharistic con-corporation (a co-bodily union): the bride receives the impress of the bridegroom's sacrificial body, which transforms her once and for all. Washed by the rain of his blood and immersed in it – a rhetorical posture she declares in the *Letters* ("I Catherine, servant and slave of the servants of Jesus Christ, write to you in His precious Blood") – she begins to speak in his name, becoming Christ's avatar in the religious sense: the embodiment of divine consciousness and will.

Thus, the first act is a gnoseological discipline: it reconfigures self-perception towards knowledge of God and culminates in unitive love. The second is a conformative action: it literally embodies the vision of love and gives birth to love of neighbour. Catherine herself explains this dynamic: "The soul" – she says – "begins by exercising herself... in the ordinary virtues, remaining in the cell of self-knowledge, in order to know better the goodness of God towards her". Once she has recognised it, "she loves it ... without the medium of herself ... and with the medium of virtue, which she has conceived through love of [God]" (Catherine of Siena 1907: 17, 27). Once the soul "has conceived by the affection of love, she immediately is delivered of fruit for her neighbor, because, in no other way, can she act out the truth she has conceived in herself, but, loving [God] in truth, in the same truth she serves her neighbor" (Catherine of Siena 1907: 27).

Catherine's case is an extreme instance of avatar production: a radically transformative experience that reconfigures the senses, 'immersing' them in God, so that everything is remembered, known, seen, touched, and felt only in God:

> Through this vision of love – increasing from day to day – the soul is so transformed into God..... Itself and other creatures it sees only in God, itself and others it remembers only in God. Thus, it is like a man who dives into the sea and swims under water: all he can see and touch is water and the things in the water, while, as for anything outside the water, he can neither see it nor touch it nor feel it. (Raymond of Capua 2003: 86)

The embodiment of vision shows that the specificity of the medieval avatar lies in presupposing an anti-fictional, immersive production of presence that couples the discipline of senses and emotions with the concrete practice of action.

Granted, the psychagogic, psychosomatic, and performative dimensions of this process make full sense within the theological anthropology of medieval Christianity. Nevertheless, they offer a trans-historical lens for understanding the complex, individual-and-collective negotiation of perception at work in modern and contemporary representation

References

Note on citations: Patristic works are cited in-text by work and locus only (no critical edition) and are not listed here; unpublished manuscripts are cited only in footnotes; all primary sources analysed and cited are listed next.

Aelred of Rievaulx. (1971a). '*De institutione inclusarum*'. In *Aelredi Rievallensis Opera omnia*. Edited by Anselm Hoste & Charles H. Talbot, 635–682. Turnholti: Brepols.

—— (1971b). 'A Rule of Life for a Recluse'. In *Treatises; The pastoral prayer*. Translated by Mary Paul Macpherson, 41–102. Kalamazoo: Cistercian.

Alzati, Cesare. (2005). 'La Liturgia come sistema di percezione del Tempo'. In *Tempo dei santi tra Oriente e Occidente: Liturgia e agiografia dal tardo antico al concilio di Trento*. Edited by Anna Benvenuti & Marcello Garzaniti, 15–29. Roma: Viella.

Apollonio, Mario. (1956). *Storia, dottrina, prassi del coro*. Brescia: Morcelliana.

Asad, Talal. (1993). *Genealogies of Religion: Discipline and Reasons of Power in Christianity and Islam*. Baltimore: Johns Hopkins University Press.

Augustine. (2003). *Expositions of the Psalms, 99–120*. Translated by Maria Boulding. Edited by Boniface Ramsey. III/19. New York: New City Press.

Bartolomei Romagnoli, Alessandra. (2021). 'Girard e il Dio delle vittime: mistica e sacrificio alla fine del medioevo'. In *Donne e sacro. Forme e immagini nel cristianesimo occidentale*. Edited by Adelaide Ricci, 103–133. Roma: Viella.

Bartolomei Romagnoli, Alessandra, Massimo Vedova, & Raffaele Di_Muro, eds. (2024). *La croce nel primo secolo francescano: scritture immagini modelli*. Spoleto: Fondazione Centro italiano di Studi sull'alto Medioevo.

Bettetini, Maria. (2004). *Figure di verità. La finzione nel Medioevo occidentale*. Torino: Piccola biblioteca Einaudi.

Bino, Carla. (2008). *Dal trionfo al pianto. La fondazione del 'teatro della misericordia' nel Medioevo (secc. V–XIII)*. Milano: Vita e Pensiero.

—— (2015). *Il dramma e l'immagine: teorie cristiane della rappresentazione*. Firenze: Le lettere.

—— (2019). 'Le lectiones latine del codice "Illuminati" e il Planctus Magistrae Doloris'. In *Teatro Sacro: Pratiche di dialogo tra religione e teatro*. Edited by Pier Maurizio Della Porta & Alessandro Tinterri, 95–145. Perugia: Morlacchi.

(2020). 'Schema/Typos. Alcuni appunti sui significati di figura nella teoria cristiana della rappresentazione'. *Mantichora. Italian Journal of Performance Studies* 10: 77–87.

(2021a). 'Baci, lacrime e unguenti. Maddalena ai piedi di Cristo nella rappresentazione passionata cistercense'. In *Donne e sacro. Forme e immagini nel cristianesimo occidentale*. Edited by Adelaide Ricci, 65–86. Roma: Viella.

(2021b). 'Per un'indagine dei significati di repraesentare nel pensiero cristiano. Alcuni esempi tra retorica e liturgia (XI-XII secolo)'. In *Presenza-assenza: meccanismi dell'istituzionalità nella 'Societas Christiana' (secoli IX-XIII)*. Edited by Guido Cariboni *et al.*, 29–42. Milano: Vita e Pensiero.

(2023). 'A "Dramatic Turn": The Revolution of Christian Representation.' In *Performing the Sacred: Christian Representation and the Arts*. Edited by Carla M. Bino & Corinna Ricasoli, 32–46. Leiden: Brill.

(2024a). 'Bonaventura drammaturgo del "dramma della passione"'. In *Bonaventura autore spirituale*. Edited by Marco Guida & Daniele Solvi, 41–49. Firenze: Edizioni del Galluzzo.

(2024b). 'Il "teatro" francescano della croce. Liturgia e devozione'. In *La Croce nel primo secolo francescano: scritture, immagini, modelli*. Edited by Alessandra Bartolomei Romagnoli *et al.*, 309–328. Spoleto: CISAM.

(2025). 'La "simplicitas" come dispositivo anti–finzionale'. In *Giullare di Dio. Lo sguardo rovesciato sul mondo di Francesco d'Assisi*. Edited by Carla Bino & Nicolangelo D'Acunto, 135–149. Roma: Carocci.

Bleumer, Hartmut. (2012). 'Immersion im Mittelalter: Zur Einführung'. *Zeitschrift für Literaturwissenschaft und Linguistik* 42 (3): 5–15.

Bonaccorso, Giorgio. (2013). *L'estetica del rito: sentire Dio nell'arte*. Cinisello Balsamo: San Paolo.

Boquet, Damien. (2005). *L'ordre de l'affect au Moyen Âge: autour de l'anthropologie affective d'Aelred de Rievaulx*, Publications du CRAHM. Caen: Centre de recherches archéologiques et médiévales.

(2017). 'Affectivity in the Spiritual Writings of Aelred of Rievaulx'. In *A Companion to Aelred of Rievaulx (1110–1167)*. Edited by Marsha Dutton, 167–196. Leiden: Brill.

Boquet, Damien, & Piroska Nagy. (2018). *Medieval Sensibilities: A History of Emotions in the Middle Ages*. Translated by Robert Shaw. Cambridge: Polity.

Brantley, Jessica. (2007). *Reading in the Wilderness: Private Devotion and Public Performance in Late Medieval England*. Chicago: University of Chicago Press.

Braumann, Georg. (1976). Morphe. In *Dizionario dei concetti biblici del Nuovo Testamento*. Edited by Lothar Coenen *et al*. Bologna: Edizioni Dehoniane.

Brufani, Stefano. (1989). 'La fraternita dei disciplinati di S. Stefano.' In *Le fraternite Medievali di Assisi. Linee storiche e testi statutari*. Edited by Ugolino Nicolini *et al*., 45–86. Assisi: Accademia Properziana del Subasio.

Butler, Cuthbert. (1951. *Western Mysticism: The Teachings of SS Augustine, Gregory, and Bernard on Contemplation and the Contemplative Life*. London: E. P. Dutton.

Bynum, Caroline Walker. (1982). *Jesus as Mother: Studies in the Spirituality of the High Middle Ages*. Berkeley: University of California Press.

(1995). *The Resurrection of the Body in Western Christianity, 200–1336*. New York: Columbia University Press.

(2011). *Christian Materiality: An Essay on Religion in Late Medieval Europe*. New York: Zone Books.

(2020). *Dissimilar Similitudes: Devotional Objects in Late Medieval Europe*. New York: Zone Books.

Cariboni, Guido. (2011). *Il nostro ordine è la Carità. Cistercensi nei secoli XII e XIII*. Milano: Vita e Pensiero.

Carruthers, Mary J. (1990). *The Book of Memory: A Study of Memory in Medieval Culture*. Cambridge: Cambridge University Press.

(1993). 'The Poet as Master Builder: Composition and Locational Memory in the Middle Ages'. *New Literary History* 24 (4): 881–904.

(1998). *The Craft of Thought: Meditation, Rhetoric, and the Making of Images, 400–1200*. Cambridge: Cambridge University Press.

(2018). '"The Desert", Sensory Delight, and Prayer in the Augustinian Renewal of the Twelfth Century'. In *Prayer and the Transformation of the Self in Early Christian Mystagogy*. Edited by Hans van Loon *et al*., 393–407. Leuven: Peeters.

Casagrande, Carla. (2015). 'Le emozioni e il sacramento della penitenza'. In *Passioni dell'anima teorie e usi degli affetti nella cultura medievale*. Edited by Carla Casagrande & Silvana Vecchio, 305–325. Firenze: SISMEL-Edizioni del Galluzzo.

(2025). 'Feelings and the Saving of Souls: Penance and Prayer'. In *Managing Emotions in the Middle Ages*. Edited by Flocel Sabaté, 41–61. Leiden: Brill.

Casetti, Francesco. (2023). *Screening Fears. On Protective Media*. New York: Zone Books.

Catherine of Siena. (1907). *The Dialogue of the Seraphic Virgin, Catherine of Siena*. Translated by Algar Thorold. London: K. Paul, Trench, Trübner.

Chazelle, Celia. (2001). *The Crucified God in the Carolingian Era: Theology and Art of Christ's Passion*. Cambridge: Cambridge University Press.

Chen, Andrew. (2018). *Flagellant Confraternities and Italian Art, 1260–1610: Ritual and Experience*. Amsterdam: Amsterdam University Press.

Cillerai, Beatrice. (2008). *La memoria come capacitas Dei secondo Agostino: unità e complessità*. Pisa: ETS.

Coccia, Emanuele. (2009). 'Il canone della passione. Il pathos di Cristo tra antichità e medioevo'. In *Le sujet des émotions*. Edited by Damien Boquet & Piroska Nagy, 123–161. Paris: Beauchesne.

Cohen, Esther. (1995). 'Towards a History of European Physical Sensibility: Pain in the Later Middle Ages'. *Science in Context* 8 (1): 47–74.

Costa, Beniamino, Leonardo Frasson, & Giovanni M. Luisetto, eds. (1979). *S. Antonii Patavini Sermones dominicales et festivi: ad fidem codicum recogniti*. 3 vols. Vol. 1. Padova: Edizioni Messagero.

D'Acunto, Nicolangelo. (2010). 'Bonifacio VIII, Assisi e il Sacro Convento'. *Bullettino dell'Istituto Storico Italiano per il Medio Evo* 112: 311–323.

De Capitani, Franco. (2018). 'Medicina, disciplina, misericordia. La cura del corpo e dell'anima come espressione dell'amore del prossimo e di Dio nel giovane Agostino antimanicheo (Mor. Eccl. 27,52–28,58 ss.).' *Rivista di Filosofia Neo-Scolastica* 110 (3): 547–562.

De Dominicis, Federico. (2024). 'Maria spasmata e Maria palmata: la rappresentazione di Maria sotto la croce in uno scritto pseudobonaventuriano (e pseudo-rabaniano)'. In *Bonaventura autore spirituale*. Edited by Marco Guida & Daniele Solvi, 259–274. Firenze: SISMEL.

Delio, Ilia. (1999). 'Bonaventure and Bernard: On Human Image and Mystical Union'. *Cistercian Studies Quarterly* 34 (2): 251–263.

Dietz, Elias. (2022). 'Aelred on Lent and Holy Week'. *Cistercian studies quarterly* 57 (1): 31–43.

Dutton-Stuckey, Marsha. (1983). 'Getting Things the Wrong Way Round: Composition and Transposition in Aelred of Rievaulx's De Institutione Inclusarum'. In *Heaven on Earth: Studies in Medieval Cistercian History*. Edited by Ellen Rozanne Elder, 90–101. Kalamazoo: Cistercian.

Dutton, Elisabeth M., & Racha Kirakosian. (2023). *Dramatic Wardrobes: The Dynamics of Clothing in Mystical Visions and Religious Plays*. Zürich: Chronos.

Dutton, Marsha L. (1992). 'The Face and Feet of God: The Humanity of Christ in Bernard of Clairvaux and Aelred of Rievaulx'. In *Bernardus Magister*. Edited by John R. Sommerfeldt, 203–223. Kalamazoo: Cistercian.

Eugeni, Ruggero. (2012). 'First Person Shot: New Forms of Subjectivity between Cinema and Intermedia Networks'. *Anàlisi: quaderns de comunicació i cultura*: 19–31. https://doi.org/10.7238/a.v0iM.1499.

——— (2018). 'What Time Is in? Subjective Experience and Evaluation of Moving Image Time'. *Reti, saperi, linguaggi, Italian Journal of Cognitive Sciences* 1: 81–96.

Falvay, David. (2025). 'The Passion Narrative in the *Meditationes Vitae Christi*: Texts and Images'. In *Communicating the Passion: The Socio-Religious Function of an Emotional Narrative, 1250–1530*. Edited by Pietro Delcorno & Holly Johnson, 101–120. Turnhout: Brepols.

Ferri, Riccardo. (2007). *Gesù e la verità. Agostino e Tommaso interpreti del Vangelo di Giovanni*. Roma: Città nuova.

Fischer-Lichte, Erika. (2008). *The Transformative Power of Performance: A New Aesthetics*. Translated by Saskya Iris Jain. New York: Routledge.

Flora, Holly. (2010). 'Empathy and Performative Vision in Oxford Corpus Christi College MS 410'. *Ikon: A Journal of Iconographic Studies* 3: 169–177.

Foucault, Michel. (1994). *Dits et écrits, 1954–1988*. Edited by Daniel Defert & François Ewald. 4 vols. Vol. 3. Paris: Gallimard.

Frank, Thomas. (2011). 'Gli statuti dei Disciplinati di S. Stefano di Assisi. Nuova edizione'. In *Statuti, matricole e documenti*. Edited by Giovanna Casagrande et al., 9–116. Perugia: Deputazione di storia patria per l'Umbria.

Fulton Brown, Rachel. (2002). *From Judgment to Passion: Devotion to Christ and the Virgin Mary, 800–1200*. New York: Columbia University Press.

Gehl, Paul F. (1987). '"Competens Silentium": Varieties of Monastic Silence in the Medieval West'. *Viator* 18: 125–160.

Gertsman, Elina, ed. (2008). *Visualizing Medieval Performance: Perspectives, Histories, Contexts*. Burlington: Ashgate.

——— (2015). *Worlds Within: Opening the Medieval Shrine Madonna*. University Park: The Pennsylvania State University Press.

Ginzburg, Carlo. (1999). *Holzaugen über Nähe und Distanz*. Translated by Renate Heimbucher. Berlin: Wagenbach.

Guijarro, Susana. (2013). 'The Monastic Idea of Discipline and the Making of Clerical Rules'. *Journal of Medieval Monastic Studies* 2: 131–147.

Gumbrecht, Hans Ulrich. (2004). *Production of Presence: What Meaning Cannot Convey*. Stanford: Stanford University Press.

Gunn, Cate, & Liz Herbert McAvoy. (2017). *Medieval Anchorites in Their Communities*. Cambridge: D.S. Brewer.

Hadot, Pierre. (1993). *Exercices spirituels et philosophie antique*. Paris: Institut d'études augustiniennes.

Hamburger, Jeffrey F. (1998). *The Visual and the Visionary: Art and Female Spirituality in Late Medieval Germany*. New York: Zone Books.

Hamburger, Jeffrey F., & Anne-Marie Bouché, eds. (2006). *The Mind's Eye: Art and Theological Argument in the Middle Ages*. Princeton: Princeton University Press.

Hardison, Osborne Bennett Hardison Jr. (1965). *Christian Rite and Christian Drama in the Middle Ages: Essays in the Origin and Early History of Modern Drama*. Baltimore: Johns Hopkins University Press.

Haubrichs, Wolfgang. (2003). 'Emotionen vor dem Tode und ihre Ritualisierung'. In *Codierungen von Emotionen im Mittelalter*. Edited by Charles Stephen Jaeger & Ingrid Kasten, 70–97. Berlin: de Gruyter.

Herbert McAvoy, Liz. (2011). *Medieval Anchoritisms: Gender, Space and the Solitary Life*. Woodbridge: D.S. Brewer.

Herbert McAvoy, Liz, & Mari Hughes-Edwards. (2005). *Anchorites, Wombs and Tombs. Intersections of Gender and Enclosure in the Middle Ages*. Cardiff: University of Wales Press.

Hofmann, Hasso. (1974). *Repräsentation: Studien zur Wort- und Begriffsgeschichte von der Antike bis zum 19. Jahrhundert*. Berlin: Duncker & Humblot.

Johnson, Eleanor. (2019). *Staging Contemplation: Participatory Theology in Middle English Prose, Verse, and Drama*. Chicago: The University of Chicago Press.

Johnson, Holly. (2012). *Grammar of Good Friday: Macaronic Sermons of Late Medieval England*. Turnhout: Brepols.

Jones, Edward Alexander. (2012). 'Rites of Enclosure: the English Ordines for the Enclosing of Anchorites, s. XII–s. XIV'. *Traditio* 67: 145–234.

Jørgensen, Hans Henrik Lohfert, Laura Katrine Skinnebach, & Henning Laugerud, eds. (2023). *Animation between Magic, Miracles and Mechanics: Principles of Life in Medieval Imagery*. Denmark: Aarhus University Press.

Karnes, Michelle. (2011). *Imagination, Meditation, and Cognition in the Middle Ages*. Chicago: The University of Chicago Press.

Kessler, Herbert L. (2019). *Experiencing Medieval Art*. Toronto: University of Toronto Press.

Kiening, Christian. (2019). *Mediality in the Middle Ages: Abundance and Lack*. Translated by Nicola Barfoot. Leeds: ARC Humanities Press.

Kinsley, David Robert. (1987). Avatāra. In *The Encyclopedia of Religion*. Edited by Mircea Eliade & Charles Joseph Adams. New York: Macmillan.

Knox, Dilwyn. (1994). 'Disciplina: le origini monastiche e clericali del buon comportamento nell'Europa cattolica del Cinquecento e del primo Seicento'. In *Disciplina dell'anima, disciplina del corpo e disciplina* della società tra medioevo ed età moderna. Edited by Paolo Prodi, 63–99. Bologna: Il Mulino.

Köster, Helmut. (1979). Splagchnizomai. In *Grande lessico del Nuovo Testamento*. Edited by Gerhard Kittel & Gerhard Friedrich. Brescia: Paideia.

Kubartová Poláčková, Eliška. (2023). *Medieval Laments of the Virgin Mary: Text, Music, Performance, and Genre Liminality*. Amsterdam: Amsterdam University Press.

L'Hermite Leclercq, Paulette. (1999). 'Aelred of Rievaulx: The Recluse and Death According to *Vita Inclusarum*'. *Cistercian Studies Quarterly* 34 (2): 183–201.

La Salle, Donald G. (1997). Liturgical and Popular Lament: A Study of the Role of Lament in Liturgical and Popular Religious Practices of Good Friday in Northern Italy from the Twelfth to the Sixteenth Centuries'. PhD Dissertation, Catholic University of America.

Lagerlund, Henrik, ed. (2007). *Representation and Objects of Thought in Medieval Philosophy*. Aldershot: Ashgate.

Largier, Niklaus. (2007). *In Praise of the Whip*. Translated by Graham Harman. New York: Zone Books.

— (2022). *Figures of Possibility: Aesthetic Experience, Mysticism, and the Play of the Senses*. Stanford: Stanford University Press.

Leclercq, Jean. (1957). 'Disciplina'. In *Dictionnaire de spiritualité ascétique et mystique, doctrine et histoire*, 3, 1291–1302. Paris: Beauchesne.

— (1961). *The Love of Learning and the Desire for God: A Study of Monastic Culture*. New York: Fordham University Press.

— (1962). 'La flagellazione volontaria nella tradizione spirituale dell'occidente'. In *Il Movimento dei disciplinati nel settimo centenario dal suo inizio*, 73–83. Perugia: Deputazione di Storia Patria per l'Umbria.

Lia, Pierluigi. (2007). *L'estetica teologica di Bernardo di Chiaravalle*. Firenze: Edizioni del Galluzzo.

Loraux, Nicole. (1990). *Les Mères en deuil*. Paris: Éditions du Seuil.

Lugaresi, Leonardo. (2008). *Il teatro di Dio. Il problema degli spettacoli nel cristianesimo antico (II-IV secolo)*. Brescia: Morcelliana.

Mancia, Lauren. (2019). *Emotional Monasticism: Affective Piety in the Eleventh-Century Monastery of John of Fécamp*. Manchester: Manchester University Press.

— (2025). *Embodied Epistemology as Rigorous Historical Method*. Cambridge: Cambridge University Press.

Maranesi, Pietro. (2005). 'Il Verbum Crucifixum: un termine risolutivo della «Theologia Crucis» di S. Bonaventura?' *Doctor Seraphicus* (52): 79–113.

Marrow, James H. (1979). *Passion Iconography in Northern European Art of the Late Middle Ages and Early Renaissance. A Study of the Transformation of Sacred Metaphor into Descriptive Narrative*. Kortrjik: Van Ghemmert.

Marx, William. (2025). 'Emotions and Orthodoxy in Medieval Latin Devotional Writing'. In *Managing Emotions in the Middle Ages*. Edited by Flocel Sabaté, 62–79. Leiden: Brill.

Maude, Kathryn. (2021). *Addressing Women in Early Medieval Religious Texts*. Cambridge: Brewer.

Mauss, Marcel. (1935). 'Les techinques du corps.' *Journal de psychologie normal et pathologique* 32 (3–4): 271–293.

Mazza, Enrico. (2007). 'Liturgia come anamnesis: una nozione da riesaminare?' *Didaskalia* 37 (2): 13–26.

McNamer, Sarah. (2010). *Affective Meditation and the Invention of Medieval Compassion*. Philadelphia: University of Pennsylvania Press.

Melville, Gert. (2025). 'Francesco e i frati Minori. Una istituzionalità ribaltata? Riflessioni su tre episodi'. In *Giullare di Dio: Lo sguardo rovesciato di Francesco d'Assisi sul mondo*. Edited by Carla Bino & Nicolangelo D'Acunto, 19–29. Roma: Carocci.

Merback, Mitchell B. (2007). 'Living Image of Pity: Mimetic Violence, Peace-Making and Salvific Spectacle in the Flagellant Processions of the Later Middle Ages'. In *Images of Medieval Sanctity: Essays in Honour of Gary Dickson*. Edited by Debra Higgs Strickland, 135–180. Leiden: Brill.

Michael, Pavulraj. (2016). '"Avatar" and Incarnation: Gita Spirituality and Ignatian Spirituality at the Crossroads'. *Gregorianum* 97 (2): 323–342.

Milanese, Guido Fabrizio. (2024). 'Conversion. A Tale of Three Etymologies'. *Lingue antiche e moderne* 13: 55–84.

Miles, Margaret. (1983). 'Vision: The Eye of the Body and the Eye of the Mind in Saint Augustine's "De trinitate" and "Confessions"'. *The Journal of Religion* 63 (2): 125–142.

Mills, Robert. (2005). *Suspended Animation. Pain, Pleasure and Punishment in Medieval Culture*. London: Reaktion.

Mondzain, Marie-José. (2003). *Le commerce des regards*, L'ordre philosophique. Paris: Éd. du Seuil.

Morrison, Karl F., & Rudolph M. Bell. (2013). *Studies on Medieval Empathies*. Turnhout: Brepols.

Muessig, Carolyn. (2002). *Preacher, Sermon and Audience in the Middle Ages*. Leiden: Brill.

Nagy, Piroska. (2000). *Le don des larmes au Moyen Âge: un instrument spirituel en quête d'institution (Ve-XIIIe siècle)*. Paris: Editions Albin Michel.

(2022). 'Événement et émotion collective. Le cas des Flagellants à Pérouse (1260)'. In *Histoire des émotions collectives épistémologie, émergences, expériences*. Edited by Damien Boquet *et al.*, 133–162. Paris: Classic Garnier.

Nelson, Robert S. (2007). 'Empathetic Vision: Looking at and with a Performative Byzantine Miniature'. *Art History* 30 (4): 489–502, 658–659.

Nerbano, Mara. (2015). 'Le rappresentazioni della settimana santa. Dall'elaborazione del repertorio testuale al teatro materiale (XIV–XVI sec.)' In *La scena materiale. Oggetti e pratiche della rappresentazione nel teatro medievale*. Edited by Tiziano Pacchiarotti, 263–318. Alessandria: Edizioni dell'Orso.

(2017). 'Appendice. Inventari delle confraternite di S. Stefano e di S. Lorenzo'. In *Il Laudario 'Illuminati' e la costellazione assisiate*. Edited by Francesco Santucci *et al.*, 303–317. Perugia: Deputazione di storia patria per l'Umbria.

Newhauser, Richard G. (2014). *A Cultural History of the Senses in the Middle Ages*. London: Bloomsbury Academic.

Newman, Barbara. (2005). 'What Did It Mean to Say "I Saw"? The Clash between Theory and Practice in Medieval Visionary Culture'. *Speculum* 80 (1): 1–43.

Nouzille, Philippe. (2011). 'Temps et liturgie. Présence et représentation'. *Collectanea Cistercensia* 73: 174–186.

O'Daly, Gerard J. P. (1987). *Augustine's Philosophy of Mind*. Berkeley: University of California Press.

Oexle, Otto Gerhard. (1976). 'Memoria und Memorialüberlieferung im früheren Mittelalter'. *Frühmittelalterliche Studien* 10 (1): 70–95.

Olson, Vibeke. (2017). 'Blood, Sweat, Tears, and Milk. "Fluid" Veneration, Sensory Contact, and Corporeal Presence in Medieval Devotional Art'. In *Binding the Absent Body in Medieval and Modern Art*. Edited by Emily Kelley, 11–31. London: Routledge.

Palazzo, Éric. (2014). *L'invention chrétienne des cinq sens dans la liturgie et l'art au Moyen âge*. Paris: Éditions du Cerf.

Palumbo, Lidia. (2008). *Mimesis. Rappresentazione, teatro e mondo nei dialoghi di Platone e nella 'Poetica' di Aristotele*. Napoli: Loffredo.

Panofsky, Erwin. (1927). '"Imago Pietatis": Ein Beitrag zur Typengeschichte des "Schmerzensmanns" u. d. "Maria Mediatrix"'. In *Festschrift für Max J. Friedländer zum 60. Geburtstage*, 261–308. Leipzig: Seemann.

Parrinder, Geoffrey. (1997). *Avatar and Incarnation: The Divine in Human Form in the World's Religions*. Oxford: Oneworld.

Patrick, Henriet. (2019). '*Murus silentii*. La construction de l'intériorité par le silence, de Grégoire le Grand à Pierre Damien'. In *Le discours mystique entre Moyen Âge et première modernité. I La question du langage*. Edited by Marie-Christine Gomez-Géraud & Jean-René Valette, 204–229. Paris: Honoré Champion.

Pellegrini, Paolo. (2013). *Planctus Magistrae Doloris. Volgarizzamento in antico veronese: testo critico, note e commento linguistico*. Berlin: De Gruyter.

Penna, Romano. (2002). 'Il concetto biblico di "verità". Alcuni aspetti semantici'. *PATH–Pontificia Accademia Theologica* 1 (2): 203–219.

Pentcheva, Bissera Vladimirovna. (2010). *The Sensual Icon: Space, Ritual, and the Senses in Byzantium*. University Park: University of Pennsylvania press.

Perrone, Lorenzo. (2006). '"The Bride at the Crossroads": Origen's Dramatic Interpretation of the Song of Songs'. *Ephemerides Theologicae Lovanienses* 82: 69–102.

Perugi, Maurizio, & Gina Scentoni, eds. (2007). *Il laudario assisano 36 dall'Archivio di San Rufino*. Perugia: Deputazione di Storia Patria per l'Umbria.

Pickering, Frederick P. (1970). *Literature & Art in the Middle Ages*. Coral Gables: University of Miami.

Pinotti, Andrea. (2020). 'Avatars. Shifting Identities in a Genealogical Perspective'. In *Shifting Interfaces: An Anthology of Presence, Empathy, and Agency in 21st-Century Media Arts*. Edited by Hava Aldouby, 31–45. Leuven: Leuven University Press.

(2023). 'The Avatarization of the (Self)Portrait. Notes Towards a Theological Genealogy of the Virtual Self'. In *Reconfiguring the Portrait*. Edited by Abraham Geil & Tomáš Jirsa, 190–204. Edinburgh: Edinburgh University Press.

Raymond of Capua. (2003). *The Life of St. Catherine of Siena*. Translated by George Lamb. Rockford: TAN Books and Publishers.

Ries, Julien, ed. (1993). *Expérience religieuse et expérience esthétique. Rituel, art et sacré dans les religions*. Louvain-la-Neuve: Centre d'Histoire des Religions.

Rosenwein, Barbara H. (2006). *Emotional Communities in the Early Middle Ages*. Ithaca: Cornell University Press.

Rosenwein, Barbara H. (2015). *Generations of Feeling: A History of Emotions, 600–1700*. Cambridge: Cambridge University Press.

Sanmartín Bastida, Rebeca. (2023). *Staging Authority: Spanish Visionary Women and Images (1450–1550)*. Alessandria: Edizioni dell'Orso.

Santi, Francesco. (2020). 'Maria che abbraccia il corpo morto di Gesù. Il tema della passione di Cristo tra Bernardo di Clairvaux e Bonaventura da Bagnoregio'. In *L'eletta dello Spirito: Maria in Bonaventura*. Edited by Letterio Mauro, 3–11. Milano: Edizioni Biblioteca Francescana.

Saxer, Victor. (1959). *Le Culte de Marie-Madeleine en Occident des origines à la fin du Moyen-Age*. Paris: Clavreuil.

Scarcez, Alicia. (2014). 'The Proto-Cistercian Office for Mary Magdalene and Its Changes in the Course of the Twelfth Century'. In *Mary Magdalene in Medieval Culture. Conflicted Roles*. Edited by Robin Waugh & Peter Loewen, 51–74. New York: Routledge.

Scarry, Elaine. (1985). *The Body in Pain: The Making and Unmaking of the World*. New York: Oxford university press.

Schembri, Gennaro. (1969). 'The Penitential Act at the Beginning of the Mass in the "Ordines Romani"'. *Melita Theologica* 21 (1–2): 52–57.

Sheth, Noel. (2002). 'Hindu Avatāra and Christian Incarnation: A Comparison'. *Philosophy East and West* 52 (1): 98–125.

Sini, Daniele. (2011). 'Il fondo diplomatico'. In *Statuti, matricole e documenti*. Edited by Giovanna Casagrande *et al.*, 169–308. Perugia: Deputazione di storia patria per l'Umbria.

Smith, Katherine Allen. (2009). 'Discipline, Compassion and Monastic Ideals of Community, c.950–1250'. *Journal of Medieval History* 35 (4): 326–339.

Starkey, Kathryn. (2004). *Reading the Medieval Book: Word, Image, and Performance in Wolfram von Eschenbach's Willehalm*. Notre Dame: University of Notre Dame Press.

Starkey, Kathryn, & Horst Wenzel. (2005). *Visual Culture and the German Middle Ages*. New York: Palgrave Macmillan.

Steenbrugge, Charlotte. (2017). *Drama and Sermon in Late Medieval England: Performance, Authority, Devotion*. Kalamazoo: Medieval Institute.

Stevenson, Jill. (2010). *Performance, Cognitive Theory, and Devotional Culture: Sensual Piety in Late Medieval York*. New York: Palgrave Macmillan.

Sticca, Sandro. (1984). *Il Planctus Mariae nella tradizione drammatica del Medio Evo*. Sulmona: Teatro Club.

Stroumsa, Guy G. (2009). *The End of Sacrifice: Religious Transformations in Late Antiquity*. Chicago: University of Chicago Press.

Terruggia, Angela Maria. (2017). 'Il laudario «Illuminati» (Assisi, Biblioteca Comunale, ms. 705)'. In *Il Laudario 'Illuminati' e la costellazione assisiate*. Edited by Francesco Santucci *et al.*, 29–90. Perugia: Deputazione di storia patria per l'Umbria.

Turner, Victor W. (1969). *The Ritual Process: Structure and Anti-Structure*. Chicago: Aldine.

Van't Spijker, Ineke. (2004). *Fictions of the Inner Life Religious Literature and Formation of the Self in the Eleventh and Twelfth Centuries*. Turnhout: Brepols.

——— (2022). *'Homo Interior' and 'Vita Socialis': Patristic Patterns and Twelfth-Century Reflections*. Turnhout: Brepols.

Van Dijk, Stephen Joseph Peter. (1963). *Sources of the Modern Roman Liturgy: The Ordinals by Haymo of Faversham and related documents (1243–1307)*. 2 vols. Vol. 2. Leiden: Brill.

Vandermeersch, Patrick. (2002). *La Chair de la Passion. Une histoire de foi: la flagellation*. Paris: Éditions du Cerf.

Weyer-Menkhoff, Stephan. (2002). 'Die Ästhetik der Liturgie'. *Liturgisches Jahrbuch* 52: 254–261.

Williams, Graham, & Charlotte Steenbrugge, eds. (2021). *Cultures of Compunction in the Medieval World*. London: Bloomsbury Academic.

Ziolkowski, Jan M. (2003). 'Amaritudo Mentis: The Archpoet's Interiorization and Exteriorization of Bitterness in its Twelfth-Century Contexts'. In *Codierungen von Emotionen im Mittelalter*. Edited by Charles Stephen Jaeger & Ingrid Kasten, 98–111. Berlin: de Gruyter.

Cambridge Elements

Histories of Emotions and the Senses

Series Editors

Rob Boddice
Tampere University

Rob Boddice (PhD, FRHistS) is Senior Research Fellow at the Academy of Finland Centre of Excellence in the History of Experiences. He is the author/editor of 13 books, including Knowing Pain: A History of Sensation, Emotion and Experience (Polity Press, 2023), Humane Professions: The Defence of Experimental Medicine, 1876–1914 (Cambridge University Press, 2021) and A History of Feelings (Reaktion, 2019).

Piroska Nagy
Université du Québec à Montréal (UQAM)

Piroska Nagy is Professor of Medieval History at the Université du Québec à Montréal (UQAM) and initiated the first research program in French on the history of emotions. She is the author or editor of 14 volumes, including Le Don des larmes au Moyen Âge (Albin Michel, 2000); Medieval Sensibilities: A History of Emotions in the Middle Ages, with Damien Boquet (Polity, 2018); and Histoire des émotions collectives: Épistémologie, émergences, expériences, with D. Boquet and L. Zanetti Domingues (Classiques Garnier, 2022).

Mark Smith
University of South Carolina

Mark Smith (PhD, FRHistS) is Carolina Distinguished Professor of History and Director of the Institute for Southern Studies at the University of South Carolina. He is author or editor of over a dozen books and his work has been translated into Chinese, Korean, Danish, German, and Spanish. He has lectured in Europe, throughout the United States, Australia, and China and his work has been featured in the New York Times, the London Times, the Washington Post, and the Wall Street Journal. He serves on the US Commission for Civil Rights.

About the Series

Born of the emotional and sensory "turns", Elements in Histories of Emotions and the Senses move one of the fastest-growing interdisciplinary fields forward. The series is aimed at scholars across the humanities, social sciences, and life sciences, embracing insights from a diverse range of disciplines, from neuroscience to art history and economics. Chronologically and regionally broad, encompassing global, transnational, and deep history, it concerns such topics as affect theory, intersensoriality, embodiment, human-animal relations, and distributed cognition. The founding editor of the series was Jan Plamper.

Cambridge Elements

Histories of Emotions and the Senses

Elements in the Series

Boredom
Elena Carrera

Marketing Violence: The Affective Economy of Violent Imageries in the Dutch Republic
Frans-Willem Korsten, Inger Leemans, Cornelis van der Haven and Karel Vanhaesebrouck

Beyond Compassion: Gender and Humanitarian Action
Dolores Martín-Moruno

Uncertainty and Emotion in the 1900 Sydney Plague
Philippa Nicole Barr

Sensorium: Contextualizing the Senses and Cognition in History and Across Cultures
David Howes

Zionism: Emotions, Language, and Experience
Ofer Idels

Affective Touching: Neurobiology and Technological Applications
Mark Paterson

Embodied Epistemology as Rigorous Historical Method
Lauren Mancia

Making Sense of Knowledge: Feminist Epistemologies in the Greek Birth Control Movement (1974–1986)
Evangelia (Lina) Chordaki

Disenchanting the Senses: Sulfuric Discourse and the World System
Andrew Kettler

Outdoor Singing in Modern Britain: A Sensory and Emotional History
Abbi Flint and Clare Hickman

Medieval Avatars: Projecting Presence, Performing Emotions
Carla Maria Bino

A full series listing is available at: www.cambridge.org/EHES

For EU product safety concerns, contact us at Calle de José Abascal, 56–1°,
28003 Madrid, Spain or eugpsr@cambridge.org.

www.ingramcontent.com/pod-product-compliance
Lightning Source LLC
LaVergne TN
LVHW011856060526
838200LV00054B/4360